GENESIS I—II

GENESIS 1–11
Tales of the Earliest World

A New Translation and Essays by
Edwin M. Good

STANFORD UNIVERSITY PRESS
STANFORD, CALIFORNIA

Stanford University Press
Stanford, California

Printed in the United States of America on acid-free, archival-quality paper

Library of Congress Cataloging-in-Publication Data
Bible. O.T. Genesis I-XI. English. Good. 2011.
Genesis 1-11 : tales of the earliest world / Edwin M. Good.
pages cm
Includes bibliographical references.
Translated from the Hebrew.
ISBN 978-0-8047-7496-3 (cloth : alk. paper) —
ISBN 978-0-8047-7497-0 (pbk. : alk. paper)
1. Bible. O.T. Genesis I-XI—Commentaries. I. Good, Edwin M. (Edwin Marshall),
1928- translator, writer of added commentary. II. Title. III. Title: Genesis one to eleven.
BS1233.G66 2011
222'.11077—dc22
2011004863

Typeset by Bruce Lundquist in 10.5/15 Adobe Garamond

Cover image: FIAT LUX by Imelda Almqvist, www.imelda-almqvist-art.com. *Fiat lux* is
Latin for "Let there be light," a phrase from the creation story in Genesis 1. A fresco by
Giusto de Menabuoi in the baptistery of the cathedral of Padua inspired this painting.

For Anita,
with love and gratitude

רבות בנות עשו חיל
ואת עלית על־כלנה

Contents

Preface

This book had an origin somewhat unusual. I was having a conversation one evening with my wife, Anita Sullivan, about the creation story in Genesis, chapter 1, not a regular subject of conversation between us. Afterward, I thought that I ought to look again at the Hebrew text. Doing so, I was pleased to find that my knowledge of Hebrew, though somewhat rusty, had not completely abandoned me, and I thought I'd just try a bit of translating. Coming up for air several days later, I realized that I had drafted about twenty-five pages of a book that looked to turn into a reading of the first eleven chapters of Genesis. And here it is, mercifully slender and the product of some rather unaccustomed thinking about things I had not thought about for some time. When I retired from Stanford University in 1991, I thought I had published my last book about the Hebrew Bible, a sizable one on the Book of Job (*In Turns of Tempest: A Reading of Job with a Translation*, Stanford University Press, 1990). Well, I was mistaken.

If I read Genesis, chapters 1–11, with as much attention as I can, it may be one way to persuade those who read this discussion to do the same with their own eyes and minds. My point is not to set forth the Final Truth about these chapters. I am pretty well convinced that there is no Final Truth to them, which is not to say that they have no truth in them. But sometimes truth makes its way most persuasively by being unfamiliar. Or a proposal's very unfamiliarity allows a reader to stop and ponder closely what she thinks—or has previously thought—is true. Then if she decides that she thinks something different from me, the thought may well be more precise, more focused, than it was before. One of my aims is to assist people to read with care and to make up their own minds more clearly.

Early in a long career of teaching at Stanford University, working with most amazing students and faculty colleagues in many fields of study, I had knocked out of me any notion that my duty was to turn them into my intellectual clones. That experience has spilled over into how I feel about readers of what I write, and this book is perhaps even more centered on that kind of presentation. Not that I will be shy about saying what I think. But I deeply desire readers to understand that my intention is not to provide them with a predigested "true perception" of these stories, but to show what in my own ways I have perceived. I have no difficulty with the idea that one outcome of that reading may be a level of disagreement with me. Fine. Use your own eyes and mind with all their capabilities and qualities, and see what you see. And I hope you will notice how many of my sentences end with question marks.

In fact, one of the surprises in pushing my way through the thickets of these chapters was how my perceptions have changed since I wrote earlier on the same material. There are some statements here that I could not have made twenty or thirty years ago. On the present trip through these texts I saw a good many things that I simply never noticed before, and I think some of them were for me at those times unthinkable thoughts. Other things I thought back then prevented my seeing some of what I see now. I am grateful to whatever elements of life and experience have made possible such change.

Edwin M. Good
Eugene, Oregon

Acknowledgments

Colleagues from various eras and segments of my career have given friendly, extremely helpful comments and answers to questions on earlier drafts: James S. Ackerman, Robert Ashbaugh, Richard Berg, David J.A. Clines, Burke Long, Marion T. Merrill, John Nicols, Arden Shenker, Steven J. Weitzman, Deborah Westbrook. None of them is responsible for any of the interpretations or ideas in the book, but all have assisted me to improve the presentations. One of the special advantages of my having married a writer is that Anita Sullivan has given me generous, sometimes properly acerbic, responses to several drafts. Her worth, as an old Hebrew proverbmonger once said, is "far beyond rubies."

GENESIS I–II

INTRODUCTION

I have written on these chapters before, both in my first book (which I leave unnamed, preferring that people not look up what I now consider a youthful production, from whose positions I have mostly departed) and in my second, *Irony in the Old Testament* (1965; second edition, 1981).

Thinking about the Hebrew Bible throughout my academic career and since my retirement, I have come to think of it centrally with that title, and not how I was first trained to know it: as the Old Testament. I am very conscious of its "Hebrewness" and its antiquity, its setting in a culture so different from ours that we would be quite helpless if transported into it. As the Old Testament, it is the first volume of a two-volume Christian book, and a great many people suppose they are very comfortable with reading Christian books. The New Testament, however, is also the product of an ancient culture, or a combination of them, Jewish, Greek, and Roman, of the first centuries of the Common Era. As products of their times, both volumes think in unfamiliar ways.

Many are quick to gloss over this strangeness, partly because there is a long theological tradition of a doctrine of divine inspiration, which says that God made the book so it would bring us truth. Well, perhaps, but in the twenty-first century it is no longer comfortably familiar, for example, to use the metaphor of a shepherd for the deity. I know there are still shepherds to be found in our country. In a long life, I have never actually met one, and I doubt that many of my readers have. We have some sentimental paintings that we suppose represent what shepherds do, but their sentimentality is misleading. Moreover, the constant use of the term "Lord" for both the deity and Christ has come to us from cultures immersed in structures of kingship and aristocracy, where what "Lords" were, or even "lords," was well known. We are not bound in such structures anymore, and the metaphor of a "Lord" or "King" is an anachronism. The kings (or queens) in our own day are without political power. I will not suppress evidence from the ancient world of the use of such metaphors for the divine. But I prefer to translate "The LORD is my shepherd" as "Yahweh is my shepherd," and that may propose some healthy unfamiliarity. In any case, I do not suppose that readers are Christian, and I hope that many are Jewish and any other current persuasion or nonpersuasion. It seems to me that recent decades have newly seen the Bible, whether Hebrew or Christian, as an artifact in the public and secular possession rather than as the exclusive property of the pious.

My issue in any case is not the search for contemporary relevance. As a longtime student of antiquity, I am most impressed by the fact that the Hebrew Bible, and therefore the book of Genesis, was not written for us. I suspect the thought that their work might ever be translated into any other language never came to the storytellers' minds. Though I have tried to translate the Hebrew text in a way that will be intelligible to contemporary readers, it is nevertheless important to me to help you realize that even in an English translation, you are reading an ancient Hebrew book.

Nor is this in any common sense a "Jewish" book. Only in the last centuries before the Common Era was there a religious culture that could sensibly be called Jewish. Before much of the earlier Israelite population was effectually removed from its homeland in the eighth century B.C.E. by the Assyrians (think "the ten lost tribes"), the nation was "Israel," and following the Babylonian invasion of the remaining territory of the tribe of Judah in the sixth century B.C.E., it was mostly a province of one foreign empire after another. In any case, "Jew" means a member of the tribe of Judah. So my effort here is to assist your entry into an ancient culture to see how it did what it did with some of its tales and its lore.

Some readers may wonder why I have stopped at the end of chapter 11 of Genesis. It is not as arbitrary as it might seem. With chapter 12 begins the story of the nation of Israel, focusing on several generations of that tribally constituted nation's prime ancestors, Abraham, Isaac, Jacob, and Joseph. The first eleven chapters focus on the world's beginning (the "earliest world" of the book's subtitle), dealing with the whole world's people, as they understood it, rather than with a people who would be a distinctive nation and culture. Those chapters, then, form a frequently identified prologue to the story of Israel itself, from the creation to the birth of Abraham and the beginning of his migration from Mesopotamia to what became Palestine.

In the interest of entry to that ancient culture, I have made a number of decisions about translating and interpreting. I have made my own translation of the Hebrew text, which is in many details somewhat different from other translations. For one thing, my policy is to avoid what I think are inadequately demonstrated meanings of words. If I concluded that I could not figure out what a given word meant, I have left an ellipsis (...) where the word ought to be, with a note explaining it. There are not many of these. In one or two instances I have used the same ellipsis to stand for a word that is clearly not applicable in the context and could be made relevant only by changing the Hebrew text. I have a longstanding policy against changing any consonant in the Hebrew text—I explain this in more detail later—although I freely change vowels. In some places it seems clear that one or more words somehow dropped out of the Hebrew text in the course of its being copied, probably in the early Middle Ages. The same ellipsis stands for those gaps.

I have decided to use the Hebrew words for the deity, mostly Elohîm and Yahweh (or Yahweh Elohîm). The English habit, ever since the King James Version of 1611, of representing Yahweh, the Israelite god's proper name, as "the LORD" (and in 1611 the English translators knew quite intimately what a "lord" or a "Lord" was) descends from the relatively early Jewish sense that the name of the deity was too holy to pronounce. I do not wish to run offensively in the face of that theological principle, but as I feel that it applies only to devout Jews, which I am not, I dare to hope that devout Jews will not give up on reading this book but will mentally make the right substitution. Moreover, I am dissatisfied to use the English word "God" to represent Elohîm. I think that too many readers assume they know what "God" means, and I am convinced that what the word means to most of us, Christian, Jewish, or other, in twenty-first-century America does not come near to matching what *Elohîm* meant to ancient Israelites. So I use the Hebrew words, and if they are void of connotations to English readers, that is fine. I hope readers will not just carry their assumptions about what "God" means to these words, but if they do, there is not a whole lot I can do about it.

These two words, Elohîm and Yahweh, later occur in patterns that suggest they represent varying strands of the traditional tales they are being used to tell. It is not necessary now to discuss exactly how they represent that, but you will notice, I hope, that Elohîm is the only term for the deity used in chapter 1 of Genesis, and Yahweh Elohîm is the only one used in chapter 2 from verse 4 on. And when we get to the two interwoven Flood stories, one of the observations by which they can be disentangled is the presence in what I call Flood 1 of Yahweh, and in Flood 2 of Elohîm. Additional observations besides those are necessary to analyze the two stories. These two narrative strands probably represent somewhat differing viewpoints as well as differing times in Israel's history when they took their current forms. We need not drive a wedge between Elohîm and Yahweh by suggesting that Israelites thought of them as different gods. It's somewhat more like the different styles of talk and prayer, for example, that can be observed among various Christian churches or among different branches of Judaism.

Still another departure from translational convention is the presentation of proper names of characters in the stories. I have decided against using the often mistaken English versions of them. So you will see, for instance, Chavah (*ch* as in Bach) instead of Eve; Hebel instead of Abel; Qayin (the *q* without a following *u* is pronounced like *k* quite far back in the throat) instead of Cain; and Nōach instead of Noah. Part of the point is the reminder that you are reading a Hebrew book, with odd-looking, foreign-sounding names instead of familiar names, many of which have been transported into our own language and usage (I know people named Eve and Jared and Noah). Many names were brought into English from German, which explains why so many of our accustomed names with Hebrew origins have *j*'s in them. German pronounces written *j* as English pronounces *y*, so Yephet is what you will see here instead of Japheth. I hope these unfamiliar spellings assist some other possibly unfamiliar aspects of the texts to come through.

One of the standard complaints about Hebrew prose style is that nearly every sentence begins with "And." There are even books in the Hebrew Bible that begin with "And." Some translations prefer to bow to an English stylistic prejudice against beginning every sentence with "And," but I have decided to be more literal. It is possible that in a couple of cases I failed to notice my omission of an "And," and I dare to hope you'll forgive it.

Finally, and most important, unlike my earlier published entries into these chapters, I have decided not to engage here in debates with or references to other scholars who have written about the material. It's not because I suppose that others, such as Robert Alter (he comes first to mind, because we are both centrally concerned with the literary qualities of biblical texts), have thought badly about these chapters; it is merely that I am trying to bring my own eyes and mind to bear as closely as I can to this material. I have, of course, consulted dictionaries and grammars of classical Hebrew. And in search of facts that have not stuck in my head (what is the length of a cubit?), I have consulted standard dictionaries of the Bible, which give that kind of information. I have even dared to ask a couple of questions about Hebrew usage to some colleagues in the field. But I have not searched out recently published articles and books on Genesis to discover the current state of the scholarly discussion. Having been at work on other kinds of research subjects, I have not been for some years closely in touch with the scholarship of the Hebrew Bible.

I have expanded on a number of points in the text in notes, which are arranged at the end of the book. These notes are designated in the text by superscripted letters, for example, [a].

In short, I have not had in the front of my mind scholarly readers, who know and follow the discussions of scholars. They are, of course, welcome to notice their own or competing positions on various aspects of the text and to cheer or grumble as their inclinations suggest. Instead, I am thinking mostly of their students or their friends, of whatever persuasions, as my prospective readers—and of my wife, a discussion with whom was the original inspiration for this writing, and who, though a superb reader and writer, does not regularly enter the Bible in any of its guises. I very much hope that many readers are like her.

CHAPTER I

GENESIS IN SEVEN DAYS

Our name of the book of Genesis comes from Greek, and it means "origin, beginning." The Israelites named their books from the first words in them, and the Hebrew name for Genesis is *Berē'šît*, "In beginning" (I explore the word more below). The account in 1.1–2.4 is the first of two creation stories, probably a later understanding than the second story.

This account is a very formal tale, structured clearly and consistently around seven days. Its way of going about its work within that structure is also very formal, and so is its rather repetitive literary style. Elohîm (we'll see a different way of referring to the deity in ch. 2) says that something is to happen, and it happens: "'Let light be.' And light was" (v. 3). Elohîm looks at what he has done and pronounces it good. Then he names the thing or things created, and the day ends. There are, of course, specific ways of dealing with various happenings on a given day. Matters seem to get a bit more extensive as the chapter moves along, and at its end is a specific application of all of this to Israel's life. We look first at the translation of the text itself, and then I discuss some of its interesting and important aspects.

Finally, the often repeated word "good" has significant connotations in Hebrew, not only of excellence in general, or of high morality, but also of beauty. As you see the constant refrain "it was good" throughout this story, you might have that sense of "beautiful" in mind, especially at the very last remark when, with everything finished, Elohîm looks at all he has done and thinks that it is "very good."

In the translations, boldface numbers refer to the chapter in Genesis; superscripts are verse numbers.

1   ¹When Elohîm began to create[a] the sky and the earth, ²the earth was shapeless and empty[b] and darkness across the abyss, and Elohîm's wind[c] swept across the waters. ³And Elohîm said, "Let light be." And light was. ⁴And Elohîm saw the light, that it was good. And Elohîm made a division between light and dark. ⁵And Elohîm called the light Day, and the dark he called Night. And it was evening and it was morning day one.[d]

⁶And Elohîm said, "Let a bowlshape[e] be in the middle of the waters, and let it make a division between waters and waters." ⁷And Elohîm made the bowlshape, and it made a division between the waters that were underneath the bowlshape and the waters that were above the bowlshape. And it was so. ⁸And Elohîm called the bowlshape Sky. And it was evening and it was morning a second day.

⁹And Elohîm said, "Let the water underneath Sky be gathered into one place, and let the dry appear." And it was so. ¹⁰And Elohîm called the dry Earth, and the gathered water he called Sea. And Elohîm saw that it was good.

¹¹And Elohîm said, "Let Earth produce green, plants seeding seed, fruit trees making fruit by their kinds, in which is their seed on Earth." And it was so. ¹²And Earth brought out green, plants seeding seed by their kinds, and trees making fruit in which is their seed by their kinds. And Elohîm saw that it was good. ¹³And it was evening and it was morning a third day.

¹⁴And Elohîm said, "Let there be lightgivers in the bowlshape of Sky to make division between Day and Night, and let them be for portents

and for set times and for days and years. ¹⁵And let them be as lightgivers in the bowlshape of Sky, to give light on Earth." And it was so. ¹⁶And Elohîm made the two big lightgivers, the Big Lightgiver to rule Day and the Small Lightgiver to rule Night, and the stars. ¹⁷And Elohîm placed them in the bowlshape of Sky to give light upon Earth, ¹⁸and to rule Day and Night and to divide between light and dark. And Elohîm saw that it was good. ¹⁹And it was evening and it was morning a fourth day.

²⁰And Elohîm said, "Let the waters swarm swarms of living things, and let flyers fly over Earth, across the surface of the bowlshape of Sky." ²¹And Elohîm created the huge sea monsters and all the living things that creep,ᶠ with which the waters swarm, by their kinds, and all winged flyers by their kinds. And Elohîm saw that it was good. ²²And Elohîm blessed them, saying, "Be fruitful and multiply and fill the waters in Sea, and let flyers multiply in Earth." ²³And it was evening and it was morning a fifth day.

²⁴And Elohîm said, "Let Earth produce living things by their kinds, cattle and creepers and wild beasts by their kinds." And it was so. ²⁵And Elohîm made the wild beasts by their kinds and the cattle by their kinds and all the creepers on the ground by their kinds. And Elohîm saw that it was good. ²⁶And Elohîm said, "Let us make humans in our image, according to our likeness, and let them dominate the fish of Sea and the birds of Sky and the cattle and all Earth and all creepers that creep on Earth." ²⁷And Elohîm created humans in his image, in Elohîm's image he created them, Male and Female he created them. ²⁸And Elohîm blessed them, and Elohîm said to them, "Be fruitful and multiply and fill the Earth and subdue it, and dominate the fish of Sea and the birds of Sky and all the living things that creep on Earth."

²⁹And Elohîm said, "There now,ᵍ I have given you all the green seeding seed that is on the surface of all Earth, and all the trees in which is the fruit of trees seeding seed; it is yours for food, ³⁰and to all the wild beasts and to all birds of Sky and to all creepers on Earth in which is living being, all the green plants for food." And it was so. ³¹And Elohîm saw all that he had made, and, there, it was very good. And it was evening and it was morning a sixth day.

2   ¹And Sky and Earth and all their hosts were finished. ²And Elohîm finished on the seventh day his work that he had done. And he rested on the seventh day from all his work that he had done. ³And Elohîm blessed the seventh day and made it holy, because in it he had rested from all his work that Elohîm had created to do.

⁴This is the history^h of Sky and Earth when they were created.

A later writer in Greek knew this story well, and decided to imitate it for his own purposes: "In the beginning"—he did know this story—"was the word" (John 1.1). Not only did he know it, but he understood it after his fashion. It is a creation story focused on words. Everything that Elohîm does is first spoken. "'Let light be.' And light was." The speech, it seems, causes the deed. And when the deed is done, and Elohîm ponders the result, speech is reported again: "And Elohîm called the light Day, and the dark he called Night." Having named Day, Elohîm has completed the first day.

There is a peculiarity about *Elohîm*, this designation of the deity: it is a masculine plural noun, the singular of which was probably *Eloah*, which occurs often in the Book of Job, or perhaps more familiarly *El*, which is found often elsewhere in the Hebrew Bible, as well as in some surrounding cultures. But this plural noun regularly takes, here and elsewhere, singular verbs, unusual for Hebrew, which usually matches plural verbs to plural nouns. Some thinkers believe that the plural form expresses the idea that this god is the final and perfect deity, though I do not find other instances of the use of a plural to denote perfection. There is no way to be certain of the idea or of its reality. This deity was clearly the only one to whom the Israelites were supposed to pay attention. But there are a couple of places later that look as if the storytellers may have been thinking of plural Elohîm.

This story of creation is shown in a process of abstractions that, by naming, become concrete or familiar things or forces. It starts with darkness, but then there is light, and Elohîm proceeds to name them both, Day and Night. Then we go to the abstract "bowlshape," which divides in two the waters that were already there, and Elohîm names that object Sky.

One apparent abstraction may not be one. The first Hebrew word, usually translated "in the beginning," poses a somewhat esoteric and difficult problem of grammar. The way the word is written, it says not "in *the* beginning" but "in beginning of," the natural continuation of which would be "Elohîm's creating." That requires modifying the traditional written form of the verb "create," which for those who know Hebrew is in a perfect tense, the masculine singular *bara'*. Along with a number of others, I have translated it as, "When Elohîm began to create," a more English way of saying, "In the beginning of Elohîm's creating," making the verb "create" by a change of vowels into an infinitive form, *b^{e}rō'*. If that seems a radical thing to do, the fact is that the Hebrew of the Bible, until the Middle Ages, was written entirely in consonants, and one was supposed to figure out what word and form a given collection of consonants would likely come out to. In our case, *bara'* and *b^{e}rō'* would have looked exactly the same, as their consonants, *br'*, are the same. Moreover, one had learned in the synagogue school what the words were considered to be through memorizing them. Languages change over time, as do the understandings of texts. Vowel signs were added to the biblical text in the Middle Ages, and they represent the way the words were pronounced in the synagogue services. To modify the vowels that were added in the Middle Ages is not at all a radical thing to do. To propose changing a consonant, however, is more radical, and I try never to do it.

It seems clear that the storytellers were not thinking of what later philosophical and theological traditions, speaking Latin as they often did, called *creatio ex nihilo*, "creation from nothing," namely, that the creator was not working with preexisting stuff. But in this story, something was there—the empty, shapeless "earth," darkness, the "abyss," the wind across waters. The latter is, by the way, I'm convinced, really wind, Elohîm's wind. Most Christian translations turn the word into "spirit," often capitalized. That strikes me as deciding on the basis of Christian Trinitarian theology a translation of what the biblical text—the basis of Christian theology, if theologians are to be believed—says and means. I'm not satisfied to do that. The theology needs to be based on what the text says as it says it—which does not ease theology's job (but theology is not my job). The verb for the wind's action, which I have translated "swept," has sometimes been rendered as "brooded." It's an interesting image, but the verb is rare enough not to allow very wide interpretive boundaries.

After light comes to be, the next thing is to put something new in the middle of something old, the bowlshape in the middle of the waters. You may notice that "waters" has a plural form, which it has in Hebrew, though there are some odd things about it. Hebrew has singular and plural forms for its nouns but also "dual" forms, meaning two of whatever is being named, often for "eyes," "hands," feet," and other pairs. The word for "waters" is odd in being accentuated as if it were dual. A dual form might refer to the two bodies of water, above the bowlshape and below it.

"Bowlshape" may strike you as peculiar, but we are dealing here with that pattern of beginning with abstractions, which are then named as familiar objects; "light" to "Day" and "dark" to "Night," for instance. The Hebrew word *raqîaʿ*, then, ought to refer to something abstract, and "bowlshape" is the closest I can come to it. The Hebrew word is rather rare, and some authorities suggest that sometimes it refers to something like a thin, beaten, metal plate. It is evidently solid, which is why some earlier translations used the word "firmament." I take it to be like an upside-down hemisphere, and we'll see it again in the Flood story. It comes to be named "Sky," and I urge you not to think of that as the equivalent of "heaven," even though many translations render it as "heaven." On occasions when the Hebrew Bible refers to it as where the deity lives, that may have a meaning something like "heaven," though heaven was not for the ancient Israelites a place to which people went after death. They went to a place always called Shᵉʾōl, which was thought of as being below the Earth.

Then Elohîm concentrates on half the waters, those underneath Sky, and moves them into one place; and where they once were, something dry appears. He names that dry stuff Earth, and the waters take the name Sea. So the creation continues from the abstract to the specific, though it is still at a high level of abstraction. So far darkness and waters have had added to them: first light, then a shape that appears to be a hemisphere, which has water both above and beneath it, and then a separation under that hemisphere of water from the dry. We will hear more about the waters that are above Sky and below Earth in the Flood story. But we need to notice here that Earth appears to be a self-contained, hollow object surrounded on all sides by water. It is also interesting that the water that forms Sea is all in one place. The Israelites had no idea that the world contained more than one ocean. To be sure, in fact the world does contain only one ocean, which receives different names in its different parts, but from any one of which you can ride a ship into another. But the Israelites, not being a seagoing people, were not knowledgeable about the sea. Nor were any other ancient peoples aware of the size and extent of the ocean.

One omission, odd to us, is that what fills the space between Earth and the bowlshape of Sky is never mentioned. The Israelites seem never to have thought of air as a substance, though they knew about wind and clouds and rain and such, as well as breath. In fact, as far as I can tell, there is no classical Hebrew word for air apart from "wind."

Now Elohîm separates the waters from what is first described as "dry"—most English translations call it here "dry land," but that is premature. The Hebrew simply says "dry" as an abstraction, and Elohîm names it Earth. Like Sea, Earth is all in one place—again, the ancient Israelites, like most of the ancient world, had no idea of the existence of several separated continents. And Earth is now instructed to "produce" something abstractly "green." Thus Elohîm does not "make" or "create" the plants, it seems, but Earth produces them. The green is then categorized into two sorts, plants that sow their seed and plants that bear fruit with seed in it. So we have a classification—what botanists call a taxonomy, an abstract category divided into its components—of the greenery in terms of the ways the plants reproduce themselves. Again, however, notice that it is first the abstract "green" and then the concrete "plants" in their two subdivisions, each of which has its "kinds," or species, as we would think of them.

Then Elohîm turns to Sky, and puts what are abstractly called "lightgivers" there. The word is related to but distinct from the original word for light, the first thing created. That light in Hebrew was *'ôr*, but a lightgiver is *ma'ôr*, a verbal noun having a causative sense. A *ma'ôr* gives light, causes it to be light. So these lights are derivative of the original, abstract light. This may very well upset our modern minds, because we know perfectly well that what makes light for us is precisely the "lightgiver," and there is no other source of light. In *The Brothers Karamazov* Dostoevsky had his characters wonder about that, how it could be that light was created first and only on the fourth day were the sources of light created. Well, that is a problem if we take our perception and understanding of the source of light as the only way to think about it. Obviously these storytellers did not think of it that way. They were thinking about abstracts and concretes, about "light" (*'ôr*) and "lightgiver" (*ma'ôr*).

The lightgivers, too, are abstract, and when they get their names, the one we would call the Sun is the Big Lightgiver, ruling day, and the one we would call the Moon is the Small Lightgiver, ruling the night. Notice, too, that they apparently had no idea that the Moon's light is not produced by the Moon but is reflected from it to us. They supposed that the Moon, like the Sun, emitted light. Moreover, these lightgivers, including the stars, were thought of as being *inside* the solid bowlshape of Sky.

Now, Hebrew has perfectly usable words for "sun" and "moon," but they are not used here. The reason for not using those words in the story might be that the storytellers knew perfectly well that for a great many folks in territories around them—and doubtless quite a few living in their own land—the Sun and the Moon were not just lightgivers but were deities, with active roles to play in and with human life. But the lights in this story have limited duties. On the one hand, they are there as time determiners, measuring days and years but also showing "set times," sometimes translated as "seasons" and meaning something like ceremonial occasions during the year. On the other hand, they are for "portents," signals to humans of things that are happening or are about to happen. Seemingly as a kind of afterthought, the story also mentions the stars, which may strike us as strange. The stars are given no function by this story. They are just there, and that may also be an expression of an Israelite animus against the astrology that was prominent in many of the cultures around. Stars in some of those cultures were deities, but Israelites were not supposed to have anything to do with those deities. So in effect the storytellers deny that the stars have any function.

And, of course, because they are inside the hemisphere of Sky, the lights also illuminate Earth. The abstract light, the *'ôr*, may have been thought to be outside of the closed system of Sky and Earth, where there was water all around.

Having then dealt with the inanimate objects in Earth and Sky (we think of them so, though it is not entirely clear that the ancient Israelites did), Elohîm turns to living things, those that inhabit water and those that seem to inhabit Sky, everything from great (the sea monsters) to small (the "creepers"). The text says this in an oddly double way, first (v. 20) in a way that seems to mean that the Sea causes these beings to appear, that they do not result from immediate activities of the deity. He orders the Sea to "swarm swarms," and the first word, the verb, seems to be causative. As the Earth "produced" plants, so the Sea produces its inhabitants. But in v. 21 he "created" the various groups. It's almost as if what the Sea did was to produce abstractions, which Elohîm, by creating, turned into less abstract categories of beings, "sea monsters" (*tannînîm*, doubtless including whales), the "living things that creep," and the "flyers." Exactly why the "creepers" are called that is not clear, as they live in the water and doubtless were swimmers, but they were perhaps both fish and crustaceans like crabs and such. The Israelites, not being sea-goers, may not have taken the opportunity to observe sea creatures, though they were later very careful about which of them they ate. As for the "flyers," the term for them is the usual term for birds. Yet here the word is an abstractive singular, and in v. 20 is immediately followed by its cognate verb, "to fly." In v. 21 it is also singular and is accompanied by the noun for "wing," as if there might be birds that did not have wings, though in that case it might be problematic to call them "flyers." At any rate, the classifications are still relatively abstract. And we notice that Sky does not produce the birds, but somehow they are produced at the same time as the Sea creatures, perhaps to maintain the distinction of Earth, Sea, and Sky.

So Sky and Sea now have their inhabitants, lightgivers and flyers in the first, and the swarms of monsters and "creepers" in the second. And Earth has its vegetation, but not its animate inhabitants.

That happens on the sixth day. Again that curious double production turns up. In v. 24, Earth produces "living things," as did Sea, but in v. 25, Elohîm "makes" the animals. There are three classifications: cattle (*bᵉhêmah*), "creepers," and "wild beasts" (literally "living beings of land"). All three are denoted by singular abstract nouns, so they are really classes, and they include within them "kinds," species, which are not spelled out. There is, of course, no hint of an idea of evolution, which you wouldn't expect to find here. The whole thing takes place in a very short time. We may suppose that the "cattle" are the domesticated animals: sheep, goats, camels, perhaps cows. The "creepers" are perhaps the small beasts, rats, moles, and such, sometimes called "vermin." The wild beasts are out there on the land. The word for "land" here is the same as the one earlier translated "Earth," but it has connotations both of the kind of land that constitutes landscape and of the larger aggregate on which all of this happens. And again, Earth has "produced" both its vegetation and its living things (the Earth our Mother?), but Elohîm has also made them.

There is one further classification of living things on Earth, the one whose representatives considered themselves to be the apex of the entire creation and who were telling this story. (We still think of ourselves as the summit of creation, not entirely a positive thought.) They are "humans," another singular abstract noun, *'adam*, and they are, according to the story, in the very image of the deity. That in itself is a strange statement, as by the time this story was written, it was an old tradition that no statues or pictures of Elohîm were to be made. Does this say that if you want to "see" the deity, you look at human beings? It is a not impossible way of thinking of it. On the other hand, in v. 27, a somewhat different way of thinking is suggested. Like the other living things, which are subdivided into "kinds"—species, if you like—the humans are also subdivided. "Elohîm created humans in his image," and that is important enough to repeat: "in Elohîm's image he created them, Male and Female he created them." The human subdivision into "kinds" is the division into male and female, but the juxtaposition of the emphatically repeated "image of Elohîm" and "Male and Female" may also suggest that it is as male and female that humans occupy the image of the deity. The storytellers did not deal with the fact that animals are mostly male and female too, nor did they explain what they meant by putting "image" and "Male and Female" together in such a parallel sequence. But, for instance, the account leaves out any element of race or skin color or location as a subdivider of the human kind. Might there be some hint that the relationship of male and female somehow mirrors the way the deity is related to the creation? Or might the very plurality (duality, if you prefer) of the human species suggest that humans might be in the image of a plural or dual deity? There will be reason to think about this again.

A possibly difficult expression turns up here. Before this action in the creation, Elohîm has used the expression "Let there be X." Here it is different. He says, right there in Hebrew, "Let us make 'adam in our image, according to our likeness." I mentioned before that Elohîm is a noun in masculine plural form, and here we have a first-person plural verb, "let us make," and masculine plural possessive pronouns, "our image" and "our likeness." We will see some expressions like this later, and I will postpone discussion of them to that point. I would suggest not assuming that they must be instances of what we sometimes call the "royal we," as has often been used by kings and queens in the European tradition to refer to themselves. The matter may be complicated by v. 27, where the humans are said to be created "in his image," a singular pronoun. Much depends on whether we wish to emphasize the inconsistency or to pretend there is none. I call attention to the inconsistency and know no way to remove it without tampering with a consonant. The ancient Greek translation simply omitted "in his image."

There is more to this. Not only are the humans the last of the beings to be created, but they are also given the most power. In that connection, the language used is very interesting. At several points in the earlier story we have the verb "to make," 'asah; for instance, of the bowlshape (v. 7), the lightgivers (v. 16), and the land animals (v. 25). But only of certain living beings, the animals of the sea (fifth day) and the human beings, does the story use the stronger verb "create" (*bara'*). And you may notice that these two groups are the only ones who are, according to the text, "blessed" and told to "be fruitful and multiply." No doubt the land animals were expected to "be fruitful and multiply," but they were not told to do so, nor does the text mention their being "blessed." Does blessing accompany only "creating" rather than also "making"? We can go only by what the text does and does not say.

Only the humans are also told to "fill the earth and subdue it, and dominate" the other living beings. Now, that raises some problems. "Subdue" is an extremely strong verb, meaning to make others subservient, to subjugate them, even, in a couple of places elsewhere in the Hebrew Bible, to violate or rape them. It sometimes seems as if in the modern day some of us humans have set out to follow this command to the letter.

One limitation is stated, and it is seldom emphasized in interpretations of this tale. Elohîm defines what is to serve as food; it is all vegetable (vv. 29–30). All the beasts, birds, fish, and humans are to be vegetarians. That appears to be the natural order. So the subjugation of the Earth at this point in the larger story does not include the killing of any living thing for food. The Israelites did not think of plants as living things, though we do. There is no indication that the animals might kill and eat each other. So the whole creation has no carnivores. Later on, after the Flood (chs. 6–9), the range of foods is enlarged, and meat is permitted. But that is after several things seem to have gone wrong.

There is one other implied statement (1.31). Everything is now finished and ready. Where Elohîm had pronounced everything he had done before as "good," now he ponders the entire finished creation, "and there! it was very good." Elohîm is seldom an exaggerator, but I think this is a remarkably understated sentence when you consider the extent of what he has done in a very short time. And I think it worthwhile to repeat that the meaning of this Hebrew word *ṭôb*, "good," carries a connotation not merely of general excellence or of moral excellence but also of "beauty."

Then the specifically Israelite application of the creation story appears. The days have been going by, each one given its number, through six. And, by the way, there is no reason to think that the days were any longer than our approximately twenty-four hours. They are bounded and defined by sunset and sunrise, evening and morning. So it won't do, as some students of the matter have tried to do in order to bring biblical religion and science into harmony, to argue that what are called "days" actually signify geological ages. They are meant as only days, as shown by the seventh.

On the seventh day the work was finished. Slightly odd: the deity is not said to have done anything on the seventh day, but the text is clear that he "finished *on the seventh day* his work." Some ancient translations saw the inconsistency in this and changed "seventh" to "sixth." I have not followed this concern about consistency, because it is there to ponder. And don't worry if you can't figure out a way to make it consistent.

The story says that Elohîm "rested" on the seventh day, and because he did, he blessed and sanctified that day of the week. Since the verb "to rest" is *šabat*, the seventh day of the week (that is, Saturday) is called in Hebrew *shabbat*, Sabbath, the "resting." So we move from an abstraction of days by number to the named seventh day, which every reader of the story knew perfectly well was the signal day of the week, the one in which Israelites were to do no work, because Elohîm had done none, and in which, as time went on, they understood that they were to pay attention to the works of Elohîm. By the naming of the seventh day, Judaism built itself and its duties into the very fabric of the creation.

But then another, and different, creation story appears.

CHAPTER 2

THE GARDEN, PART I

2 ⁴ᵇIn the day when Yahweh Elohîm made Earth and Sky, ⁵and all the bushes of the fields were not yet there in the Earth, and all the plants of the fields were not yet growing, because Yahweh Elohîm had not made it rain on Earth, and no human was there to serve the ground. ⁶And a mist rose from the earth and wet the whole surface of the ground. ⁷And Yahweh Elohîm formed the human of dust from the ground and breathed into his nose life's breath, and the human became a living being.

⁸And Yahweh Elohîm planted a garden in Eden in the east, and there he put the human whom he had formed. ⁹And Yahweh Elohîm made to grow out of the ground all trees pleasant to look at and good for food, and the tree of life in the middle of the garden, and the tree of knowing good and evil.

¹⁰And a river came out from Eden to water the garden, and from there it divided and became four sources. ¹¹The name of the first is Pishon; it goes around the whole land of Chᵃvîlah, where there is gold. ¹²And that land's gold is good; there is bdellium and *shoham* stone.ᵃ ¹³And the name of the second is Gichon; it goes around the whole

land of Kush. [14]And the name of the third is Chiddekel; it goes east of Assyria, and the fourth is Perat.[b]

[15]And Yahweh Elohîm took the human and set him down in the garden of Eden to serve it and keep it. [16]And Yahweh Elohîm commanded the human, saying, "From all the trees of the garden you are free to eat. [17]And from the tree of knowing good and evil, you are not to eat from it, because on the day you eat from it, you will certainly die."

[18]And Yahweh Elohîm said, "The human's being alone is not good. I will make a helper for him as one facing him."[c] [19]And Yahweh Elohîm formed from the ground all the wild beasts and all the birds of Sky, and brought them to the human to see what he would name them; and whatever the human named the wild beasts, that was their name. [20]And the human gave names to all the cattle and to the birds of Sky and the wild beasts; and for Adam[d] he did not find a helper as facing him. [21]And Yahweh Elohîm made a deep sleep to fall on the human, and he slept; and he took one of his ribs and closed up the flesh in its place. [22]And Yahweh Elohîm built the rib that he had taken from the human into a woman, and he brought her to the human. [23]And the human said,

> "This one at last,
> bone from my bones,
> and flesh from my flesh.
> This one is named Woman,
> for from Man was taken this one."

[24]Therefore a man leaves his father and his mother and clings to his woman, and they become one flesh.

We notice right away several aspects in which this story is totally different from the first. The creator is now called "Yahweh Elohîm" instead of just "Elohîm." In Exodus 3.15 we learn that the deity has a proper name, which may have been pronounced "Yahweh."[e] But here that name is already in use. To pause briefly over the name, it came at some unknown point in Jewish history to be thought too holy to be actually pronounced. The holy was always felt to be potentially dangerous,

and pronouncing names might have been viewed as especially dangerous, the names of deities the most dangerous of all. Who knew what
might happen to you if you did it without the proper care? So when the
divine name Yahweh occurred in the text of the Bible, Jews came to pronounce the word *Adonai*, which means "Lord," and when in the Middle
Ages Hebrew manuscripts of the Bible came to be written with signs
for vowels, the scribes used the consonants of *Yahweh* and the vowels of
Adonai, seeming to producing the hybrid word *Jehovah*. But no one ever
said "Jehovah." Some Christian translators followed the convention, and
the King James version of the Bible, published in 1611, substituted "the
LORD" in capital letters in the Old Testament whenever the Hebrew
letters for *Yahweh* appeared. It was Christians who, being ignorant of
Hebrew, sometimes adopted *Jehovah* in translations and in theological
or other writings about the deity. We should no doubt be respectful of
Jewish feelings about this, but perhaps outside of the synagogue and
Jewish worship it is acceptable to say "Yahweh." In any case, that name
is present in this second creation story, but not in the first.

Another difference between these two is that the second story does
not have the seven-day structure that is so crucial in the first. Still another is that this tale presents the events of creation in a totally different
order. It does not show how Sky and Earth are brought into being, but
after that the first thing that happens is water to moisten the ground—
understandable in what was basically a desert climate. The first creative
action is the formation of the human (the Hebrew word is *'adam*, which
you may recognize as what later becomes the name of the first male
human, Adam). For now the word is simply a designation, and its basic
meaning is "humanity" or, in the case of an individual, "human." Then
comes the planting of the garden in Eden and the production of plants,
specifically trees of two kinds, nice to look at and good for eating, but
different categories of plants from those in the first story. As this story
does not mention any source of food but those trees that are good to
eat, we may suppose that it too describes a vegetarian world, though
that later becomes unclear. This story names two specific trees, the tree
of life and the tree of knowing good and evil. And we can hardly fail

to notice that the forbidden tree is accompanied by the threat of death. Eating it is dangerous, not because it is poisonous and will mindlessly kill you, but because Yahweh is opposed to humans having whatever benefit might come from eating it. We will return to this problem.

The garden needs some comment. To begin with, no one knows where the Israelites thought Eden had been, except "in the east" (2.8). That is general enough not to be helpful, though it reminds us that the story was being told in Palestine. I think we would do well to think of "garden" as meaning something bigger and wilder than the small, often rather formal gardens that we have in our yards. The "garden" of Eden is probably best thought of as a fairly extensive forest. Trees are the only plants mentioned in the text, though the Israelites certainly knew about underbrush in forests. The Hebrew word for "garden" carries an image of something rather beautiful, but not necessarily formal.

Then there are the rivers and the establishment of the geography of Earth, a geography bearing little relation to what we know. It is very difficult to make sense of this entire description. Nobody knows exactly what area was known as Chᵃvîlah, but Kush was used for two areas: Ethiopia or part of it, on the east coast of Africa, and an area in southeastern Mesopotamia. Ethiopia seems rather distant from Israel to be the territory meant. Assyria is perfectly well known in Mesopotamia, though the river running in the eastern part of Assyria was not, except here, called Chiddekel. We know it as the Tigris, a name derived from Persian, while the Assyrians called it Idiglat. The Perat is the Euphrates. Still, these rivers imply a strange depiction of the area.

The last creative activities involve the formation of animals (vv. 19ff), specifically in the interests of alleviating the human's loneliness. But the animals did not meet the case, and at the very last Yahweh got around to making the woman. So the entire creating process is different in this story from what it is in the first. Here there is no "let there be," only actions: "forming" the human from dustᶠ and "breathing" life into him (2.7), "planting" the garden (2.8), "placing" the man in the garden (2.15), "building" the rib into a woman (2.22). This story describes a deity who gets his hands dirty in the creating process. The only words are what Yahweh says to himself, "The human's being alone is not good," and the command he lays on the human, that he is free to eat from all the trees in the garden except one (2.16). Both of these are central statements for the progress of the story.

We shall have to return to those trees, because they become a crucial element in Genesis, chapter 3. But an indication of what is at stake here may help. Such magical trees are frequent ingredients of origin and creation stories. The "tree of life" is found more often, and it turns up again here only at the end of the garden of Eden story as a reason to exclude the humans from Eden. But there is no prohibition against eating its fruit. Why access to the tree of life is denied the humans will be looked at in the later context.

The tree of knowledge is the one that is forbidden from the outset, on pain of death. There are at least three ways of understanding the name of that tree. First, it may be thought of as the tree of knowing good and evil, where "good and evil" are the objects, the contents, of the knowledge. Exactly what that means is harder to say than it may seem. Perhaps the most obvious thing to think is that the knowledge is moral knowledge, knowledge of what acts are morally good and evil. Sometimes that interpretation leads to the perception of the activity in chapter 3 as producing the knowledge of evil, but seldom is there any indication of knowledge of good in that story. I find this account of the matter very difficult to square with the central moral thrust of the Hebrew Bible. Why would the deity, who later commands the law and requires more than mere observance of it, wish to forbid access to moral knowledge at the outset?

Second, the phrase might be thought of as the tree of "knowledge good and bad," where "good and bad" are adjectives describing the knowledge. Some knowledge is no doubt good to have; some of it may be harmful. This way of thinking of the phrase would seem to imply realms of knowledge that are moral or immoral or, perhaps, something closer to useful or not useful. Again, however, why would such knowledge as that be forbidden so stringently by the deity? We will see an argument about that question in chapter 3.

A third possibility is present. Pairs of terms like "good and evil" turn up often in the Hebrew Bible, and they are often not contrasting pairs but inclusive ones. "High and low," for instance, may signify everything in between. "Light and dark" may cover all the shades from one extreme to another. Such a pair has been given the technical term "hendiadys," derived from the Greek meaning "one through two," that is, a single subject understood through its two extremes. One thing about such pairs in Hebrew is that they almost never emphasize one of the terms over the other (I say "almost never" because I can't think of an instance, but I can't be sure that there isn't one). In this context, I think that "knowing good and evil" really means "knowing everything," perhaps more strictly "knowing everything knowable," and I will argue that point more when we get to the issue in chapter 3.

Why would Yahweh introduce such a prohibition at this point? We shall have to look at the rest of the story, and we may or may not be satisfied that the question is answered. Is it a test? "Let's see if he obeys." But why test so newly created a person, who has no experience to guide him, especially, if we can say it this way, with the issue of death? The threat of death seems somewhat strange in this context of creation. Here is the human, barely brought into being, and now he is being threatened with nonbeing. But death cannot really mean anything to him in this stage. The threat, then, must be taken to be significant to the readers, if not to the first human. Again, in chapter 3 it is brought up in the argument about the prohibition, and we'll think more about it there.

It is also necessary to say that even for Yahweh death is hypothetical. He, so far as we can see, has no experience of it either. If there is creation, bringing something into being, then there may also be "uncreation," the cancellation of the created. That would in our terms be death. Moreover, he promises *immediate* death ("on the day that you eat of it"). In the event, that does not happen. There will be much more to think about that later.

But we need to notice another difference from the first story. There the humans were put in command of the animals and Earth, and the power over Earth included a very strong term, which I translated "subdue." I noted there that this verb is sometimes used for serious abuse and even for rape. But here the human is put in the garden, as verse 15 has it, "to serve it and keep it." That sounds like the opposite of the first story, where humans were to "subdue and dominate" everything. The strong side of "serve" is to "be slave to." The noun cognate to the verb usually means "slave," sometimes merely "servant." Israelites were perfectly familiar with slaves and were not prevented from having them. To "keep" is something like guarding the garden. We will see the notion of the human as "servant" of the soil several times more. There are places where it means on the surface to "cultivate" or be a farmer. But underneath is that dimension of servitude. Thus the triumphalism of the first tale about the human function in Earth is completely different in the second.

It is an odd story in many ways, about an odd deity. As you think about Yahweh (or Yahweh Elohîm, as the text calls him), you may realize more and more that he is creating by improvisation. He had threatened immediate death for eating from the wrong tree, but in the event he did not carry out the threat. He had not thought through everything, as is further demonstrated by his remark that the loneliness of the human is "not good." It has not turned out as he may have thought it would. So he sets out to get the human a helper, and that is likewise improvised. He makes the animals and experimentally brings them to the man "to see what he would call them." There is some element of freedom in the man's activity. He is not told what to call them.

The human is involved with the animals here in a totally different way from the other story. There, humans were to be in control of the animals and of the rest of the world. Here, they are very much more on a par with the animals. In fact, the story describes them as made from the same material. The human is "formed" from dust of the ground (*'ᵃdamah*), and the animals and birds are "formed" from the ground— the same word. To give something a name is in some sense to establish a relationship with it, and in the human's naming the animals, all we know is that the names he gave stuck, but that the relationship formed thereby was not the one that Yahweh had in mind. "He did not find . . .

a helper." The subject of that verb must be Yahweh. He did not know whether he was going to find a helper for the human, but he decided to try this. Here is a creation story in which more than one thing does not turn out as the creator expected. To be sure, he decided to leave the determination of the relationship with the animals to the human. Though they were formed of the same material, which shows that the animals had a connection to him, none of them turned out to be a "helper as facing him." The Hebrew of that phrase is interesting: *ēzer kᵉnegdō* could be rendered "a helper as one in front of him." The King James version translated that in a fascinatingly appropriate way: "a helper meet for him," where "meet" means both proper for him and also one whom he meets and who meets him.

We must realize that if we are looking to find a deity who is omniscient, who knows everything, this chapter is not the one for us. This deity does not know everything, has not thought through everything, and sometimes incorrectly predicts what will happen. He was not prepared for the human's loneliness; his first effort to solve it by making animals failed, and only on his third try was the problem solved. We'll see some of this again later. But it is perhaps important to point out that ideas like omniscience and omnipotence (possessing all power) do not come to us from our Hebrew background. They come from Greek philosophy (Plato's "the One"), and we have been so imbued with those philosophical ideas that realizing they are not present in our culture's traditionally sacred book can be something of a shock. Actually, the Hebrew Bible comes closer to knowing an omnipotent deity than an omniscient one. But the philosophically pure idea of the totality is not, in my opinion, part of the Hebrew mentality. Lots of power, yes; lots of knowledge, yes. But if there was latent in the background the thought of *all* power or *all* knowledge, it is almost as if Yahweh Elohîm gives it up or at least does not use it.

The last act of the creation takes place in an interestingly dramatic way. In chapter 1 the human race was begun all at once by the divine statement, "Let us make humans in our image," which turned out to be male and female. But here is no mention of an image; the male was made first of all the creatings, and only after everything else is in place is his loneliness resolved by a surgical procedure. Anesthetic is administered in the form of not just sleep but a "deep sleep" (the Hebrew is *tardēmah*, a relatively unusual word but never ordinary sleep), followed by the extraction of a rib from the male. No, there is no gap in present male anatomy to show which rib was extracted. Not every loose end must be tied up. But when you think back to the fact that the man was made from dust, and the woman was made from bone, then you have to wonder why we have the turned-around idea that men are stronger than women. Maybe this story needs to help us overcome that idea. We men may have bigger muscles. But we are not necessarily in more important ways "stronger."

The Hebrew says that that bone is "built" into a woman. The verb is *banah*, the usual verb for building a house or anything else—another piece of physical labor in the creation. Yahweh brings her to the man, and as we men have been doing ever since, the man bursts into poetry:

> "This one at last,
> bone from my bones,
> and flesh from my flesh.
> This one is named Woman,
> for from Man was taken this one." (2.23)

How do we know this is poetry?[g] Some scholars say that Hebrew poetry is not really distinguishable from prose but tends to lie at the formal edge of prose. To recognize poetry, we must not look for the sorts of factors that define it in English or other European languages. This one has formality, a careful pairing of a three-line segment (technically called a tercet), each line of which in Hebrew has two words, followed by a two-line segment (couplet), each with three words. It has rhythm, but no strict meter. The same word, *zō't*, "this one" (feminine), is both the first and the last word of the poem, and also the first word of the couplet beginning in the fourth line. The first three lines are short, two words each, and the second and third of those lines have a certain parallelism: "bone from my bones / and flesh from my flesh." Such parallelism is a usual factor in Hebrew poetry. And then the last lines turn on a word-play, another typical occurrence in this kind of poetry: "This one is named Woman [*'iššah*—the consonant *š* pronounced *sh*] / for from Man [*'iš*] was taken this one." The word for woman, the usual feminine form of the word for man, is also the normal word used for "wife," so that one cannot tell except from the immediate context whether *'iššah* denotes simply an adult human female or a married one.

But there is a very odd, picky question of grammar there. The demonstrative pronoun "this one" (in Hebrew, *zō't*) is feminine singular, and it is preceded by a preposition, *l*ᵉ, which usually means something like "to." As I have translated the sentence, that pronoun is handled as the subject of the verb: "This one is named." The picky little point is that the verb form "is named" is passive masculine singular. So the pronoun, while it acts as if it is the subject of the verb, can't be, because Hebrew is very careful about matching the genders of its verbs and their subjects. The sentence appears to mean literally something like "To this one is given the name Woman," which is more complicated than I like to be, and the implied subject of the passive verb is indefinite. Now you are remembering, I trust—and I wish to assist your memory—that the book you are reading is an ancient Hebrew one, and the translator sometimes needs to fudge a bit to make it act sensibly in English.

We may notice a combination of approaches in this lovely little poem. On the one hand, it emphasizes the identity of man and woman: "bone" and "flesh" of the two are identical, because they have the same origin. That would point toward the possible equality of men and women. But the equality would be at the least compromised by the notice of the male's primacy; unlike the subsequent experience of humans, she came from him. Ever since then we have come from her, but in the first instance it was the opposite. And first instances often determine how people consider priorities. Unlike the first creation story, where male and female are created simultaneously by the divine statement, in the second the male is decidedly first, and the female a kind of secondary improvisation after the first attempt to alleviate loneliness fails.

A remark is in order about the various words for "man." We've now had three of them: *'adam* (chs. 1 and 2), "male" (ch. 1), and *'iš* (ch. 2). I mentioned that *'adam* means something close to "humanity" as an abstract term, though it can also, as in chapter 2, mean a single representative of the human species, and later we will even see it as a collective term for the first man and woman, with the definite article, *ha'adam*, almost "the Adam," with a plural verb. And, of course, it became a proper name, Adam, for the first man. "Male" turns up only in 1.27, when Elohîm creates the humans as "male" (*zakar*) and "female" (*n'qēbah*). There the two words specifically mean the genders, and can be used of both humans and animals. In chapter 2 we have *'îš*, "man," and *'iššah*, "woman," both of which specifically mean human men and women and are seldom used for animals.[h]

It is worth showing this poem's form by transliterating the Hebrew. I will mark accents with a mark above the accented vowel. Notice especially the word order in the concluding couplet.

> *zō't happá'am*
> *'étsem mē 'atsamáy*
> *ūbasár mibb'sarí*
> *l'zō't yiqqaré' 'iššah*
> *kî mē'îš luq'cháh zō't*

In the couplet, the second line's word order is the reverse of the first: (1a) preposition–*zō't*; (1b) verb with heavy *q* consonant; (1c) *'iššah*; (2c') "because"–preposition– *'îš*; (2b') verb with heavy *q* consonant; (2a') *zō't*; hence, a-b-c; c'-b'-a'. That poetic arrangement, where the two lines have the same words in reverse order, is called chiasmus, derived from the Greek letter X (chi). We'll see another poem later that has the same chiasmic arrangement, which is not rare in Hebrew poetry. One of the things we can usually expect in poetry, no matter what the language, is care in the arrangement and relations of the words.

Finally we are given an explanation of something that every Israelite knew, but some might not have known why it was so. Such explanations referring to origins are frequent in the mythologies of all cultures, and the specific term for this kind of explanation is "etiology." A man (*'îš*) leaves (actually, abandons) his parents and goes with his woman (*'iššah*). It is in fact stronger than that: he "cleaves" or "clings" to her.

And it seems that that verb may have more than one meaning inside it. The following statement, "and they become one flesh," suggests a literal "clinging" along with his poetic claim that she is "flesh from my flesh," already, then, "one flesh." Then their "becoming" one flesh at the end of the sentence suggests the possible if not probable sequel of their "clinging," the producing of children. There may also be a social dimension in this abandonment of father and mother. Some cultures around Israel apparently had a pattern in which, on marrying, the husband went to live with his wife's clan. Perhaps this statement indicates that at one time the Israelites did too. It is a pattern that is even now to be found, for example, in the Navajo culture in the American Southwest. In any case, this explanation brings the meaning of the creation up to date, applies it to the culture in which the story was told. It is the counterpart in this story of the Sabbath explanation of the first one.

The second creation story is entirely different, then, from the first, in its cast of characters, the order in which the creatings happen, and even the kind of language that is used. The first has a very formal and formalized language, repeating its phrases again and again, and its activities are all preceded and determined by words. This second one has much less formal, more relaxed language about the physicality of the creation, the actions, not words, that are perceived in it. The first story suggests a process of thinking through and testing what has been done ("Elohîm saw that it was good"), and there is no indication that any loose ends or less-than-perfect outcomes were considered. In the second story there are at least two experiments that do not work as the creator intended, and a command laid on the human that includes the threat of death before any human being or deity has experienced death.

It is probable that these two stories were formed at different times in Israel's history. The second story was probably the earlier one to have been composed, and it might have been circulated for many years, if not centuries, in oral form before being written down. The first story gives fairly clear indication that it came into being in writing. In fact, one strand of the scholarship on this part of the Hebrew Bible holds that the two stories are parts of two different original written documents, which were finally combined along with still other sources to form the first five books (see a brief description in Chapter Eleven, note e). I'm not sure that I can now buy that "source-critical" explanation, though I will discuss it a bit more at the Flood story. In any case, we don't really need it here, except to say that these are clearly two quite different creation stories—I take the occasion to call them myths. They meet the technical requirements to be myths, which have deities acting and speaking in them. Should anyone be offended by the word on the argument that myths are by definition untrue, I should argue the exact opposite. The word comes from a Greek word meaning simply "story" or even, as in drama, "plot." It is too bad that we have sometimes turned it into something immediately designated false. Myths are the stories taken by their cultures to be in the most important ways true: not necessarily historically or scientifically true, which requires proof of their truth, not literally true perhaps, but true for the culture's imagination, which is surely more important.

And now we move on to the events in the garden of Eden. What follows was evidently part of the same story as the one just preceding it, or the two were joined together quite early in their careers.

CHAPTER 3

THE GARDEN, PART 2

2 ^{25}And the two of them, the man and his woman, were naked, and they felt no shame.

3 ^{1}And the snake was the subtlest of all the wild beasts that Yahweh Elohîm had made, and he said to the woman, "Did Elohîm really say that you are not to eat from all the trees of the garden?" ^{2}And the woman said to the snake, "We eat from the trees of the garden, ^{3} but from the tree that is in the middle of the garden, Elohîm said to us, 'You don't eat from it and you don't touch it, lest you die.'" ^{4}And the snake said to the woman, "You're not going to die. ^{5}For Elohîm knows that on the day you eat from it, then your eyes will be opened, and you will be like Elohîm, knowing good and evil." ^{6}And the woman saw that the tree was good to eat and that it was a delight to the eyes, and the tree was desirable to bring wisdom, and she took some of its fruit and ate it and gave it also to her man with her, and he ate. ^{7}And the eyes of both were opened, and they knew that they were naked. And they sewed up fig leaves and made themselves clothes.

^{8}And they heard the sound of Yahweh Elohîm walking in the garden in the evening breeze. And the human and his woman hid from the presence of Yahweh Elohîm in the midst of the garden's trees. ⁹And Yahweh Elohîm called to the human, and said to him, "Where are you?" ¹⁰And he said, "I heard your sound in the garden, and I was afraid because I am naked, and I hid." ¹¹And he said, "Who told you that you are naked? From that tree that I ordered you not to eat from it, have you eaten?" ¹²And the human said, "That woman whom you put with me, she gave me from the tree, and I ate." ¹³And Yahweh Elohîm said to the woman, "What's this you have done?" She said, "The snake fooled me, and I ate." ¹⁴And Yahweh Elohîm said to the snake:

> "Because you did this
> cursed are you
> beyond all the cattle
> and beyond all the wild animals.
> Upon your belly you shall walk
> and dust you shall eat,
> all the days you live.
> ¹⁵And I will set enmity
> between you and the woman
> and between your descendants
> and her descendants.
> He will attack your head,
> and you will attack his heel."

¹⁶To the woman he said:

> "I will greatly increase
> your pain and childbirth.
> With pain you will bear children,
> and you will desire your man,
> but he will have charge over you."

¹⁷And to Adam he said: "Because you listened to your woman's voice and ate from the tree that I ordered you, saying, 'You don't eat from it,'

> Cursed is the ground on your account;
> in pain you will eat from it

all the days you live.
¹⁸And thorns and thistles
it will grow for you,
and you'll eat the wild weeds.
¹⁹In the sweat of your brow
you'll eat food
until you return to the ground,
for you were taken from it.
For you are dust,
and to dust you shall return."

²⁰And the human named his woman Chavah because she became the mother of all the 'living.' ²¹And Yahweh Elohîm made for Adam and his woman cloaks of leather and clothed them.

²²And Yahweh Elohîm said, "There now, the human has become like one of us, knowing good and evil. And now, lest he put out his hand and take also from the tree of life, and eat and live permanently,"ᵃ ²³Yahweh Elohîm sent him out from the garden of Eden to serve the ground from which he was taken. ²⁴And he banished the human and stationed east from the garden of Eden the cherubim and the flame of the whirling sword to guard the way to the tree of life.

The first sentence is the end of the second chapter, but it brings up a matter that will bulk large in the third. The actual but unnoticed nakedness becomes an issue as this story moves along, and it is solved only at the end of it.

And now the story becomes not only a myth, with a deity acting and speaking (and taking a walk in the evening breeze), but also a fable, the definition of which is a story in which animals speak. Not many animals speak in the Hebrew Bible. I think of only one other, the ass in Numbers 22 that the non-Israelite prophet Bil'am was riding and beating because it kept stopping for an angel, whom the ass could see but Bil'am could not. The ass complained bitterly and justly in Hebrew about being beaten because he was being sensible. Asses brake for angels.

The snake here is both talkative and described as "subtle" or perhaps "shrewd" or "canny"—the exact connotations of the word ('arūm) are not certain. But the interesting thing is that we have another pun. The Hebrew Bible is full of puns; unfortunately they can seldom be transferred into English. The word "subtle" ('arūm) is very like the word to describe the humans, "naked" ('ªrummîm, a plural form). The two words are not related, coming from different roots, but all you need for a pun is similar sound. So the subtlety of the snake somehow corresponds to the nakedness of the humans. Is it that the snake's subtlety can get through the nondefenses of the naked humans? Perhaps.

The other thing the story implies, in my opinion, is that the snake is *not* the Devil. He's only a snake, one of the wild animals, as the text says, smart, to be sure, subtle, talkative. In fact, in the outcome, the snake is punished by becoming like the snakes we know about, "walking" on his belly. The suggestion is not quite hidden that until this episode the snake had legs like the rest of the animals. It is understandable that much later, theology turned the snake into the Devil as the cause of what theology has called (the) Original Sin, but only those who need to have a Devil need to posit his presence here. I think the snake is simply another aspect of the creating that is not as Yahweh had thought it would be.

He does get through the woman's defenses. First of all, he speaks specifically to the woman, and let's not ignore the implied sexist assumption that the woman is perhaps more vulnerable than the man. Though in the end she does not receive all the punishment for this misdeed, she receives what might be seen as the worst one. The snake's subtlety shows through in the kind of question he asks, an exaggerated one. "Did Elohîm really say that you are not to eat from all the trees of the garden?" In effect, "Is what they're saying true?" We know perfectly well, because we remember what we read, that Elohîm did not say that at all. But the exaggerated question puts the woman on the defensive. "No, we eat from the garden's trees. Well, there is that one in the middle that Elohîm said not to eat or even touch, or we would die."

Now we are in the middle of something important. She said they were not to eat or touch, "lest you die." Yahweh had not mentioned touching, and had made the threat of death more serious, literally, "dying you will die," a very strong combination: "you will certainly and without recourse die on that very day." She exaggerates the prohibition and slightly underplays the threat. Perhaps we need to recall that Yahweh had made the threat to the man before she had been "built" from his rib, so she had not heard the actual words, and perhaps the man had given her this version. But the snake either has private knowledge or was listening to the conversation between the human and Yahweh—a doubtful explanation, as the conversation about eating from the trees took place, if the order of things in the story is taken as accurate, before the snake and the rest of the animals were formed: "You will not certainly die," using Yahweh's very words, *mōt tᵉmūtūn*, but adding the negative. Yahweh used the singular, *mōt tamūt*, because he was speaking only to the man; this is in the plural, because the snake is referring to the couple. And he goes on to explain why Yahweh had made what he portrays as an empty threat: "Elohîm knows that when you eat it, your eyes will be opened, and you will become like Elohîm, knowing good and evil." Elohîm is holding out on you, in other words. He has powers that you don't have, *but that you can get.*

One of the curious things about this conversation is that its participants speak only of "Elohîm," not what the narration has used, "Yahweh Elohîm." I'm not sure quite what to make of that. It is possible that a later editor of the text felt the force of the Jewish prohibition of speaking Yahweh's name. If it was too holy for pious Jews to pronounce, then it was obviously too holy for a sneaky snake recommending contravention of the divine command, or for a woman who was about to do it. Or perhaps the storytellers wanted to suggest that the snake's promise points not to the humans' becoming like the Israelite god, Yahweh, but like a more generalized god. They might even have hoped we would take the word literally, as a plural noun, meaning that the snake was suggesting a departure from the proper connection to the proper god in becoming "like gods." Interestingly, the King James Version of 1611 translated the expression in just that way. In any case, becoming like one or more deities, he suggests, includes "knowing good and evil." You'll wake up, in effect, and behold! you're gods, knowing what gods know.

It's on these levels that I think we have here a wider sense of "knowing good and evil" than the sense confined to moral knowledge. It is divine knowledge that the snake says was to be denied the humans, and divine knowledge is at least considerably beyond the scope of human knowledge. Arguing in the preceding chapter that the story does not portray an omniscient deity, I am not willing to change my mind about that here. Perhaps the most we can say is that the hendiadys "knowing good and evil" is the knowledge of everything the deity (or deities) knows. The pair "good and evil" means, then, everything from one extreme to the other. There is another statement at the end of the story that I think is even more persuasive about this reading of the phrase.

The woman ponders and perceives the values of this fruit: it is good to eat, pleasant to look at, and desirable to bring wisdom. So it is more than the other trees in the garden, which were described in 2.9 as being pleasant to look at and good for food. This one has the added excellence of promising "wisdom," and it is a reasonable possibility that the storytellers equated "wisdom" to "knowing good and evil." The woman thinks about it and makes a reasoned decision before she eats. And she hands some to the man, but he doesn't bother to think about it or even to ask which tree this came from. Just like a man—he downs whatever is set before him.

And the snake was right: they did not die, and "their eyes were opened and they knew"—not good and evil, not everything, but—"that they were naked." That is something more than they knew before and is doubtless something that Yahweh knew. Nakedness must have signified to Israelites some weakness and vulnerability. Our human pair did the best they could to cover themselves, with fig leaves. Fig leaves, of course, are rather large. But the outcome is the shame that they did not feel at the beginning. The new knowledge afforded by open eyes is not exactly what the snake had promised. Perhaps he knew better than he let on, that what they would discover was their greater weakness, not the greater power he apparently proposed. But the knowledge may imply something in addition. In 2 Samuel 19.36, in a speech that the elderly Barzillai makes to King David when the king proposes to take him to Jerusalem—for what purpose is not clear—Barzillai replies that it's no use his going to Jerusalem. He is eighty years old, and wonders, "Can I know the difference between good and evil?" He goes on that he can't even taste food and drink. Some have suggested that knowing the difference between good and evil in this passage in Samuel may have something to do with sexual ability. And that might be another aspect of what our passage has in mind. It's interesting, perhaps, that sexual knowledge or ability would seem to be an aspect of divine knowledge. Is there even more to the idea that being in the "image of Elohîm" is being male and female?

Of course, at that very moment the unexpected, dreadful thing happens: they hear the sound of Yahweh taking a nice stroll in the garden in the cool evening breeze. And their weakness is even more evident: they must hide from him, and they go as far into the thickets of the forest as they can. But it's harder to hide from Yahweh than it is for him to find them. "Where are you?" Are we to hear in that question a deity who knows perfectly well where they are? Perhaps they made a lot of noise scurrying deep into the woods. The man certainly responds immediately, admitting that hearing Yahweh walking in the garden made him afraid. Does he mean that he heard the question after he knew that it was Yahweh walking? It's not clear, as the narration uses the same "hearing" word in verse 8 to describe their hearing Yahweh walking in the garden.

The reason he is afraid is that he is naked. He has always been naked, but now he knows it in a totally new way and has tried to change it. He seems to understand now what it was that he ate. Yahweh's question is instant: "Who told you that you are naked?" Well, nobody had told him, and Yahweh seems to know that, too, without waiting for an answer: "Have you been eating that tree . . . ?"

Now starts the process of evasion, of buck-passing. "The woman," says the fellow; in fact, "that woman *you put with me* . . ." It's not only her fault and not his, but it all goes back to Yahweh himself, who gave him "that woman." The Hebrew has only a definite article, not the demonstrative "that," but I think the eloquent definite article allows a little extra emphasis. And then Yahweh turns to the woman: "What is this that you've done?" "The snake," she quickly says; "the snake fooled me, and I ate." "Fooled" may even suggest something a little stronger: "seduced." And perhaps that makes the sexual connection even more plausible.

Yahweh doesn't even invite the snake to answer a question. This cross-examination might not stand up in a modern court, but our chapter does not have a modern court. It has a deity who proceeds to lay a series of curses on the guilty parties, accepting what might seem like hearsay evidence, and going from one party to the others in reverse order.

In another indication that the snake is only a snake and not the Devil, he is reduced to wriggling along the ground instead of walking on legs, though Yahweh does use the regular verb "to walk" (*halak*). And the irony of his "walking on his belly" is that he is reduced to eating dust—that dust from which the man was made. We know that snakes do not eat dust, and perhaps the Israelites knew it too, but it was probably too good a joke to leave out. And we have another etiology, the explanation of that uneasy feeling that humans have about snakes. There is to be enmity between humans and snakes. Humans tend to want to stamp on snakes' heads, and snakes sometimes want to bite humans on the heel—the only part of the human the snake can easily reach from his prone position. But notice that the enmity is between snake and woman and their respective descendants. Is that a perception that women dislike snakes more than men do? I have seen women run for a weapon against a snake in the garden when their children are around, but I've also seen little boys proudly exhibit live garter snakes that they have caught: "Can I keep him?" Fathers are sometimes inclined to acquiesce, but I've seen very few mothers do so. This is, of course, folklore, not objective science, though lots of folklore is based on a great deal of experience and knowledge. To be sure, these storytellers wanted to connect that mutual nervousness between snakes and humans with this story, hence perhaps the claim that this was the start of it. It is a not-unexpected use of the possible truth of a myth.

The curse on the woman is really a curse against her womanhood, and I think we must recognize its presence in a sexist society. Though the term "curse" is not present in it, this poem is stated in the kind of rhetoric used in curses: "This is what will happen to you." The pain of childbirth is to be increased, though the Hebrew text first says it differently: literally the increase is of "your pain *and* your childbirth," which is then extended by "With pain you will bear children." And the sexism increases by the use of the masculine plural term for "children"; literally "with pain you will bear boys." I think the masculine plural does not mean that only the birth of boys will be painful, rather that boys were the main and decisive children in that society. Of course, there has been no childbirth experience yet to compare with the threatened increase of pain. "This is what will happen to you."

But there is more to the sexism of this curse: "You will desire your man / but he will have charge over you." Even the connection between the sexes is modified by this deed, and the woman takes the brunt of it. It seems to place in the woman's being an overweening sexual desire, a desire that is met by the man's ruling, being in charge, being the one who decides. And there was never any doubt that in Israel men were in charge. Surely this statement has issued in subsequent years in many a cruelly harsh limit placed on women's sexuality and has not discouraged men from thinking they were licensed to do anything they wished.

Nevertheless, there is also a curse involving the man, even though it does not curse *him* in so many words. Most of it has to do with the difficulty men have with farming. "Service of the ground," which was the assigned job in the second creation story, is now subject to the curse, though the words are not there. Farming has always been hard work, of course, lessened perhaps by the invention of such labor-saving devices as tractors and the like. But no one in the Near East during the Iron Age, when Genesis was transmitted, had any idea of such things. Bullocks or oxen were the most familiar labor-saving devices they knew. And the curse deals almost in more detail than anyone needs with the pain of being a farmer in a climate less than friendly to that undertaking. The curse turns on another pun, which by now should not be surprising, and which we have seen before. The man receiving the curse is *'adam*, and what is cursed on his account is the ground, the soil, *'ªdamah*. The man is reminded at the end of the curse that he was formed (2.7) out of dust from the ground (there too, *'ªdamah*). When the writers of Genesis said "dust to dust," they meant it exactly: you were formed from dust (those of you who were not formed from a man's rib), and after a life of unremitting struggle and pain, you'll go back into it. You are *'adam* and you'll end up in *'ªdamah*. This is a reminder, if one is needed, that the threat of death has been hanging in the air ever since 2.17, regardless of the snake's scoffing at the idea. To be sure, the threat of death in 2.17 included the words "on the day that you eat of it," but it takes much longer than that for death to happen. Did Yahweh not really mean what he said? Or had he not thought it through? In either case, the snake's statement was right: "you're not going to die."

The culture in which we live, coming mainly from Europe, widely believes in some form of life after death. That is an influence for us mostly of Christianity but also of Hellenistic Greece and Rome, where Christianity grew to adulthood. Christian theology pondered this story and dubbed it "the Fall," the descent of humans into what it has theologically called Original Sin, a condition that permanently damaged the human connection to the deity, until the death and resurrection of Jesus removed the taint, at least in principle. That event for Christians allowed the possibility of life after death. We need to understand, however, that Israel in the biblical period had no idea of life after death, though some forms of later Judaism adopted it.

A further descent is in store. First is some naming, reminding us of chapters 1 and 2. As he had given names to the animals in Yahweh's search for his "helper" and to the woman, the *'iššah*, now the man gives the woman the proper name Chavah. I know that in your Bible the name is Eve, but Chavah has nothing to do with evening and all its romantic softness. Her name is explained: because she "became the mother of all the living" (v. 20). It's another pun: she is Chavah, the mother of the "living" (*chay*), and Chavah means something like "life-giver." There is no specific naming of "the man," but in the description of Yahweh's making leather garments he is referred to without a definite article—not as *ha'adam*, "the human," but as Adam—which has happened before. So now they are both named and have better clothing to cover their newly aware nakedness than was afforded by fig leaves. Notice, moreover, that the leather garments that Yahweh constructs (now doing the manual work of a tailor on top of all the other manual work he did in ch. 2) are not consistent with the implied prohibition in chapter 1 of killing and eating animals, unless, of course, Yahweh made these garments from the hides of animals already dead of natural causes. Here is another little piece of evidence that the two stories really are two.

A meeting takes place before the last move in the garden, in which Yahweh makes a statement (v. 22) that may seem strange to monotheists. "There now, the human has become like one of us, knowing good and evil." The knowledge that the snake promised, "knowing good and evil," is actually acknowledged on the very highest authority. How is that connected to the "shame" and "fear" that they knew after eating the fruit? Often, when this is thought of theologically as "the Fall," it is supposed to be the awareness that they had failed, that such knowledge as they now had of good had turned evil. The Calvinists even turned that into a doctrine of total corruption—hence not the knowledge of "good and evil" but the knowledge only of evil. Ex-Calvinist that I am, I think that was a terribly mistaken reading of what was taken as the sacred text. Yahweh says, "knowing good and evil."

Who is that "us" into whose company the man has come?—and no mention is made of the woman, though she too ate from the tree; in fact she took the first bite, according to verse 6. The snake promised that the humans would be "like Elohîm, knowing good and evil," and I have remarked about that term for deity that it is masculine plural in form. And here there is no question of what is said: "The human has become *like one of us*"; or somewhat literally, "like one from us." Is there a group of gods that Yahweh addresses? Well, yes, there probably is. At a number of other places in the Hebrew Bible there is reference to a divine court, though the idea contradicts the strict notion of monotheism. Some interpreters have wanted to interpret "us" here, and also in Genesis 1.26, as the royal "we" used by many European monarchs in self-reference (recall Queen Victoria's remark at some tasteless joke, "We are not amused"). But the royal "we" is not to be found in the ancient world.

Strict monotheism, the concept that only one god exists, and all others are mere fiction, is difficult if not impossible to find in the Hebrew Bible. Israel was often bidden to have dealings with Yahweh alone, but I know no statement that must be interpreted to mean that no god but Yahweh *exists*. In fact, one of the problems the prophets in the Hebrew Bible had was that other gods than Yahweh were all too present and powerful. I have to say here that I have very slowly come to the conclusion that the Hebrew Bible is not really a monotheistic book. When it became the first volume of a two-volume Christian work and took on the name and structure of the Old Testament, perhaps at that time it was automatically read as if it were a monotheistic book. By then Judaism had become monotheistic by a process that I cannot now trace, and Christianity, as its offspring, followed suit. But when I read the Hebrew Bible strictly as it stands, I do not find monotheism a necessary tenet in it.

The conclusion from the thought that the humans were now possessed of some kind of divine knowledge is that they have to be curbed, and Yahweh proposes the simple expedient of excluding them from Eden. They must not go on having access to the tree of life. That reminds us of the intriguing fact that eating the fruit of the tree of life was never prohibited. Only the tree of knowledge was forbidden. In fact, trees of life are rather frequently found in mythologies of various cultures, and they are mostly not the kind of tree whose fruit eaten once conveys permanent life on the spot. One must be piecing at a tree of life all the time in order to maintain life indefinitely, and Adam and Chavah had clear access to it. But no longer.

The language is awfully interesting. "The human" (*ha'adam*) is the subject of all of these remarks. Sometimes, of course, *ha'adam* means the man and woman together. But the woman is not mentioned at all. Verse 23 begins: "And Yahweh Elohîm sent *him* [not *them*] out from the garden of Eden, to serve the ground from which *he* was taken, and

he banished *the human*." She went with him, of course, but the storytellers failed to include her. When *ha'adam* has a collective sense, "the
humans," it is always with a plural verb. Here both "the human" and
the verbs are singular. (One of the problems with English verbs, the sort
with which translators in my position are saddled, is that their forms are
sometimes very difficult to identify as singular or plural: "I go," "they
go," "he went," "we went." Hebrew at least allows us to know singular
from plural, and Hebrew verb forms contain the subject pronouns in
them.) But we recall that first assignment of the human, "to serve the
ground." Then it was the *'adamah* in the garden, but here he is sent away
from the garden with the same assignment, an assignment that he now
knows will be mostly pain and sorrow.

Finally Yahweh sets a guard to keep the tree of life from the whole
human race: cherubim and "the flame of a whirling sword." These are
the new guards of Eden, since the original "guard," the human, has been
sent away from it. Some translations read the cherubim as handling the
sword, but there is an "and" between them. Cherubim, by the way, are
not the cute, pudgy little angels with tiny wings in Christmas paintings
that we sometimes call "cherubs" and that are properly referred to by
their Italian name, *putti*. The ancient Cherub was an enormous com-
posite guardian figure, to be seen especially in Mesopotamia, most especially in Assyria, as a huge sculptured figure at temples and royal palaces,
with a large, bearded, helmeted human head and the body of a lion or a
bull. There are several somewhat varying descriptions of cherubim in the
Hebrew Bible (for example, in Ezekiel chapters 1 and 10), but they are
always guardians to be avoided. Our success in avoiding them is demonstrated by the fact that we have never found that tree of life. With
no clear idea even where the garden of Eden was thought to be, except
"in the east" (2.8), we may as well give it up. From now on humans live
without it, except as a distant vision of an easy life no longer available.

Whatever has happened to that constant refrain in chapter 1, "And
Elohîm saw . . . that it was good"?

Going on now to the further generations of humans, things seem
not to improve.

CHAPTER 4

OFFERINGS AND THEIR RESULTS

4 ¹And the human knew Chavah his wife, and she conceived and bore Qayin, and she said, "I have 'gotten' a man with Yahweh." ²And again she bore his brother, Hebel, and Hebel became a shepherd of the flock, and Qayin became a servant of the ground. ³And it happened, when the time came, that Qayin brought some fruit of the ground as an offering to Yahweh. ⁴And Hebel too brought some of the fattest first born of his flock. And Yahweh accepted Hebel and his offering. ⁵But Qayin and his offering he did not accept, and Qayin was very hot and his face fell. ⁶And Yahweh said to Qayin, "Why have you such heat, and why has your face fallen? ⁷Is it not that if you do well, you're raised, and if you don't do well, sin is lying in wait at the door? And it desires you, but you can take charge of it."

⁸Qayin said to Hebel his brother . . . ᵃ and it happened when they were out in the field that Qayin rose up against Hebel his brother and killed him. ⁹And Yahweh said to Qayin, "Where is Hebel your brother?" And he said, "I don't know. Am I my brother's guardian?" ¹⁰And he said, "What have you done? The voice of your brother's blood cries out to me from the ground. ¹¹And now, cursed are you from the ground, which

opened its mouth to receive your brother's blood from your hand. [12]If you serve the ground, it will no longer give you its strength. You will become a homeless wanderer in Earth." [13]And Qayin said to Yahweh, "My punishment is greater than I can bear. [14]Because you have banished me today from the ground, and I am hidden from your face, then I'll become a homeless wanderer in Earth, and anyone who finds me will kill me." [15]And Yahweh said to him, "Therefore, anyone who kills Qayin will be avenged seven times." And Yahweh put a mark on Qayin so that anyone who found him would not kill him. [16]And Qayin went away from Yahweh's presence and lived in the country of Nōd, east of Eden.

It is so typical in the Hebrew Bible that a story involving someone's birth includes a pun that explains the name. Here comes the birth of Qayin. I repeat that I'm giving transcriptions of Hebrew names in order to remind us that we're dealing with an ancient language and culture, and with characters whose names are different from the ones that have been domesticated to our language. Of course, the pun in the Hebrew doesn't work in English: Qayin, the name; *qaniti*, "I have 'gotten.'"[b]

There is an oddity about Chavah's statement "I have gotten a man with Yahweh." ("Man," by the way, is the common noun *îš*, a human male.) What could she possibly mean? Some translations turn "with Yahweh" into "with the help of Yahweh." The addition seems designed to elbow aside any thought that Yahweh might have had more than a peripheral part in the pregnancy. But the expression is odd enough to forbid certainty about its meaning. In many ancient myths, deities, especially male ones, have sexual activity with human women, but it seems not to have been a common thought in Israel. That may not be enough to forbid the thought, and we will shortly see another instance of it.

Out beyond Eden it almost looks like the Wild West, with the farmer pitted against the herdsman. Or are we too sure that there will be a competition? You'll notice that some years pass between the first and the second parts of verse 2. The chosen occupations of the brothers immediately cause trouble. The storytellers show us only what happens and do not explain why things happen as they do. Each brother brings his offering to Yahweh, Qayin's from the soil, Hebel's from the flock. Why they made offerings to Yahweh is not explained, except that "the time came." It was time for them, that's all. Of course, making offerings did not need to be explained to Israelites; it was a regular ingredient of their religion and happened on a regular schedule. What is not regular is the response. One is accepted, the other is not. Why does Yahweh set up a contest like that—or better, why does he respond to it as he does? We simply are not told. Can a deity decide something without being answerable to mere humans? Of course, we need to notice that animal sacrifice seems not compatible with the vegetarian conditions from the first creation story. But this tale involves Yahweh, not Elohîm. The next time we see sacrifice is after the Flood, and that too is sacrifice made to Yahweh. Those who told this story perhaps did not know the first creation story.

Is it a test of Qayin? It surely seems so, and he appears to take it as such. And if it is, what kind of test is it? Is it to see whether Qayin makes the correct response? If so, it is a fair test only if Qayin knows what the correct response is. Or is it to find out what response he will make? If that, then it illustrates again Yahweh's ignorance of the future, that he is searching for knowledge. Or might the test have to do with the fact that Qayin's occupation is like his father's, as a "servant of the ground"? Adam was not the most adept, it seems, as he and Chavah were expelled from Eden, to which he was supposed to have been a servant.

It should hardly be surprising that Qayin would be angry and disappointed. But the tone of Yahweh's response seems one of surprise. "Why have you such heat"—the term points to anger—"and why has your face fallen?" The metaphor of the fallen face has become familiar precisely from this passage in the English Bible, and it is an interesting one. All the contours of the face sag. But Yahweh points to an alternative: "If you do well . . ." (or do good). That might mean that Qayin failed to make his offering in the proper manner, and "doing well" would be following good ritual practice. If that was the issue, then the test depended on Qayin's knowing the proper sacrificial procedure. As this is the first sacrifice recorded, we might wonder how, in the absence of instruction, he would know. But it might mean something more like doing "good," acting in a moral way. If so, perhaps Yahweh's response proposes that doing good is more important than proper sacrifices, a somewhat startling idea in the context of Israelite religion, which put great stress on both. Some passages in some of the prophets suggest that at times and in certain circumstances Yahweh was upset by sacrifices, but that seems to be when they are not accompanied by "doing well." Again, if the test was to be a fair one, then Qayin should know what morally "doing well" entails. But we have seen no instruction in such matters.

Yahweh gives no indication that Qayin's offering was in any way wrong. He just doesn't accept it. The later sacrificial system in the Hebrew law allowed for both animal and vegetable offerings, though it seems that the animal offerings were more expensive and prestigious. Hebel was the herdsman; Qayin, the farmer. Why should that be reason enough for Hebel and his sacrifice to be accepted where Qayin and his were not? Yahweh gives no reason, and if there ever was one in the sacrificial system through which every Israelite knew and understood the story, it is not clear from any of the documents describing that system.

Yes, it looks more and more like a test, and not a very fair one. Nothing in the story indicates that either Qayin or Hebel has ever before tried to give an offering, so Qayin has no prior success with it. It seems that before he ever succeeds, he fails. "Do well, and stop worrying about the offering." Does that mean that from the start the whole sacrificial system is optional? That doing well is the only thing required? The legal passages in Exodus, Leviticus, and Deuteronomy would not suggest that, though they do not underplay the moral life either. But what constitutes doing well? How is Qayin supposed to know? There is no law in existence yet, no long tradition of ethical behavior.

Let me try a different tack. "Doing well" may have nothing to do with either sacrifices or morality. It can sometimes have a more objective meaning, entailing matters going well in life and leading to positive feelings about life. "If things are going well for you, you're lifted up," happy, pleased with your life. "But if things are not going well for you, then sin is crouching by the door"; you are in danger of attack from sin.

But "you can take charge of it." You are not, then, the victim of your circumstance. In effect, "Just get on with it."

Where did this "sin" come from anyway, to crouch like an animal in ambush by the door? This is the first—but by no means the last—use of that word in the Bible. Here it is interestingly portrayed as something outside of Qayin, not something inside him, as we often think of "sin," but as a predator that threatens to attack him. And then Yahweh repeats some words that were important in chapter 3. Sin "desires you, but you can take charge of it." Recall the curse on Qayin's mother: "You will desire your man / but he will have charge over you" (3.16). In effect, Qayin is being invited to play the man, to act as the man is expected to act with respect to the woman's cursed "desire." Sin is portrayed metaphorically, not only as an animal in ambush, waiting to snatch its prey, but also as a woman possessed by sexual desire. And the Hebrew word for "sin," *chatta't*, is a feminine noun. For the most part, it has to do with actions or thoughts that oppose the deity, but it can also mean something negative done to fellow humans. It is a very slippery concept, I think, which turns up here as a metaphor entirely without preparation or any explanation, except that it is to be controlled.

There are several possibilities of meaning in Yahweh's exhortation to Qayin—"it desires you, but you can take charge of it"—following the metaphor of the animal in ambush. The second clause is, in the nature of the Hebrew verb, not utterly straightforward. My translation, "you can take charge of it," is intended to suggest "you are in charge." But the word might mean "you will take charge," a predictive statement. Or "you must take charge," a command. Or even, "you may take charge," not "you are allowed" but "you may be able to take charge," a statement that hedges some bets, as it also implies that you may not succeed in taking charge. There is a fascinating episode in John Steinbeck's novel *East of Eden*, which took its title, of course, from this very passage. The protagonist is concerned about something he has or has not done. As the novel is set in California, he has a Chinese friend, who goes to his family organization to consult some old, wise men. Listening to his account of the problem and its connection with Yahweh's statement to

Qayin, they are interested and decide to examine the problem *by learning Hebrew*. They invite him to return several times to discuss the matter. They go through all the options of meaning in the statement, and finally conclude with the last of my options, "you may take charge"— not the one I used in the translation. It is a most interesting solution to the problem, and I am not quite convinced. In the companion passage, the curse on Chavah, there seems no question about the man's being in charge, and the most obvious meaning here would be the same, as the two sentences are virtually identical. Still, this one is part of a hypothetical situation: "If you do well . . . but if you do not do well. . . ." And perhaps that changes the meaning of the identical words to something like the contingent "you may take charge."[c] I leave the conclusion to you, and you may quite legitimately prefer any of the options I have laid out above—or others if you can think of them.

And then there is a flaw in the text: "Qayin said to Hebel his brother . . ." (4.8). What he said is missing, though some translations fudge the problem by translating "Qayin spoke to Hebel his brother," a barely possible reading, because "spoke" ought to be a different verb. Ancient translations from Hebrew into Greek, Syriac, and Latin and some Hebrew manuscripts have inserted something—or perhaps they had access to a Hebrew text that quoted Qayin. Unfortunately, the Hebrew text that has come down to us had, at some point in the copying of manuscripts, dropped Qayin's statement. The scribes were very careful in their copying, but sometimes errors crept in, and the time came when the text had been so firmly fixed and was conceived to be so holy, that even evident errors like this one could not be corrected. Clear indication of its mistake was simply part of its holiness and had to remain. No doubt Qayin said something like "Hey, let's go out to the field." Because that is what they did.

There the crime took place. Qayin killed Hebel in the great example of fratricide. Asked by Yahweh about Hebel's whereabouts (v. 9), Qayin's response has become the classic statement of moral irresponsibility. "Where is Hebel your brother?" "I don't know. Am I my brother's guardian [or keeper—or even something like what Hebel was, a shepherd]?"[d] But, as Chaucer has it ("Nun's Priest's Tale"), "Murder will out." Israelite culture apparently supposed that the ground itself would bear witness to murder by displaying the presence of bloodshed. So Yahweh says that Hebel's blood "cries aloud" from the ground. He has visited that field—or he hears sounds that are unavailable to us. Or, the most obvious solution: he used a metaphor of sound for a reality of sight.

We must notice that Qayin's question, "Am I my brother's guardian?" uses the same word as in the assignment of Adam, in the original garden, to "serve the ground and keep it," the very verb that Qayin here denies applies to him. Someone else, the cherubim, became the "guardians" of the garden when the humans were expelled, but it seems that expulsion did not exempt humans from all duties of "guarding." And here the evident correct answer to Qayin's question is "Yes, you are your brother's guardian." But since the brother is no more, Qayin loses both his guarding function and, as we will see almost immediately, his duty of service to the ground.

Another curse must be delivered. Qayin, the farmer, servant of that *ᵃdamah* from which Adam was made in order to serve it, and to which he would return, must be severed from the ground (the verb is the same one used in 3.24 of the exclusion of the humans from Eden), deprived of his living as a farmer, and made a homeless wanderer. The Hebrew expression is another assonant pair of words like "shapeless and empty" (*tōhū wavōhū*) in 1.2. This one is *na' wanad*, almost "roaming and wandering," a nomad in reality. However painful Adam's life as servant of the ground was to be because of the curse on him, Qayin is now relieved of that pain, separated from the ground, but not relieved of all pain.

Qayin fears that he will be totally helpless against anybody who might want to kill him. Why he should worry about that seems questionable in this context. He is, after all, one of only three people still on earth. Who is out there to kill him? The storytellers clearly did not worry about that, and we will shortly see another instance in which they were not concerned with such a question. But the storytellers put in a detail that has provided reason for endless useless speculation: Yahweh's putting a mark on Qayin that will somehow—how is not explained—

prevent people from killing him. What was the "mark of Qayin"? No one knows; I certainly do not, nor do I wish to. "Mark" often means a sign of something, sometimes a miraculous portent, sometimes merely a banner. And a sign or mark is as close as we will ever get. It seems another instance where the storytellers portray Yahweh as improvising, responding with an on-the-spot solution to a problem he had not previously considered. In fact, Yahweh does not say that the mark will prevent Qayin from being killed, only that if he is killed, vengeance will be sevenfold.

So Qayin departs from Yahweh's presence and lives in the country of Nōd (which means "wandering"), east of Eden. Don't try to find Nōd on any map. And don't ask too many questions about the genealogies that come next. They come out of deep tradition, and they are to be taken, I believe, as a particular kind of folklore, lore that provides a culture with named ancestors. We tend not to find such literature terribly fascinating, but I think it is because these are not our familiar ancestors. They surely became familiar ancestors to the Israelites, for whom the Hebrew Bible was written, and therefore they were in the sort of list that people were expected to know by heart. Indeed, such lists were doubtless passed down by word of mouth for a long time before they were written down.

CHAPTER 5

SOME DESCENDANTS

4 ^{17}And Qayin knew his wife, and she conceived and bore Ch^{a}nōkh. And he became the builder of a city, and he named the city by the name of his son, Ch^{a}nōkh. ^{18}And to Ch^{a}nōkh was born ʿÎrad, and ʿÎrad bore M^{c}chūyaʾēl, and M^{c}chūyaʾēl bore M^{c}tūshaʾēl, and M^{c}tūshaʾēl bore Lemekh. ^{19}And Lemekh took two wives; the name of the first was ʿAdah and the name of the second Zillah. ^{20}And ʿAdah gave birth to Yabal; he became the father of people who live in tents with herds. ^{21}And his brother's name was Yūbal; he became the father of those who handle the lyre and the flute. ^{22}And Zillah too gave birth to Tūbal-Qayin, sharpener of any implement of copper and iron; Tūbal-Qayin's sister was Naʿ^{a}mah.
     ^{23}And Lemekh said to his wives,

> ʿAdah and Zillah, hear my voice,
> wives of Lemekh, attend to what I say.
> I killed a man for wounding me,
>   a boy for bruising me.
> ^{24}If Qayin is avenged sevenfold,
>   then Lemekh seventy-seven.

[25]And Adam knew his wife again, and she gave birth to a son, and she named him Shet. "Elohîm has 'given' me another offspring in place of Hebel, for Qayin killed him." [26]And likewise to Shet was born a son, and he gave his name 'Enôsh. Then was begun invoking the name of Yahweh.

There is more like this to come, but we will pause before getting into it. This genealogy has some oddities in it, and, of course, it ends with a very brutal boast from Lemekh, and with another son and a grandson for Adam and Chavah.

Perhaps I don't need to emphasize that the fact that Qayin had a wife is very peculiar. I hope you shook your head in surprise on reading that, and thought (or even said aloud), "What?" Where did she come from, and how did Qayin find her? There is no answer to those questions. The storytellers simply did not concern themselves with it. Maybe there was once a story giving the needed details—or maybe there wasn't. There certainly isn't now. The race went on, even though the last we knew, there were only three members of it, one of them the child of the other two. Qayin got a wife (spaceship, anyone?), and off we go.[a]

Not only did Qayin get a wife, but he built a city. Who lived in it, and where did its population come from? He gave it the name of the son born of that mysterious wife (this son's name in English is usually Enoch). The city is as mysterious as Qayin's wife. If there was a city named Ch[a]nôkh, it is never referred to elsewhere, and its presumed location is completely unknown. Perhaps it was in the land of Nôd, though as a city sits in a specific location, its place in a land named "Wandering" would seem something of a contradiction in terms.

(I certainly hope that you are beginning to feel some familiarity about questions that do not have answers. I have a great many of them just in these chapters, perfectly understandable and legitimate questions to which some folks may propose answers with varying degrees of plausibility. But plausibility is not the same as knowledge or certainty, and I refuse to consider them on the same level. If you find raising questions that have no satisfactory answers uncomfortable, then I suggest that this might be a good time to give up reading this book. Because there are a lot of such questions yet to come.)

We are now told of four subsequent generations, ending with Lemekh. A small linguistic side trip may explain why some of these names don't quite match the ones in your Bible. I have noted before that ancient Hebrew was written with only consonants until the Middle Ages, when marks denoting vowels were added to manuscripts to reproduce the way the text was pronounced in the early medieval synagogues. One characteristic of those additions was that at certain points in sentences, especially the middle and last words of a sentence, a short, accented vowel was turned into a long one. (English doesn't show those in its spelling, but Hebrew does.) For instance, the first time Hebel was mentioned in the text (4.2), it was at that kind of point, and the name was spelled in Hebrew as Habel. When that was carried over into Latin and then to English, it became Abel. The same thing happened to Lemekh at the very end of 4.18, appearing as Lamekh, Englished as Lamech. But at the beginning of 4.19, as in the second half of 4.2, the correct, ordinary spelling of both names has an *e* in the first syllable, Hebel and Lemekh. Now you know more about the spelling of Hebrew names than you wanted to, and I have told you merely in case you wondered why I misspelled Abel's and Lamech's names. I didn't.

With Lemekh's offspring some strange possibilities occur. 'Adah his wife produces two sons with somewhat similar names, Yabal and Yūbal. Names in Hebrew mean something, and are often reasons for interesting research. Yabal becomes a nomadic herdsman, it seems. Living in tents is not strange, but the text says literally "Living in tents and herds." It makes it sound as if Yabal had a large bunch of relatives living in herds around his tents. But Yabal's name is related to a noun, *yōbēl*, which means "ram." Yūbal, on the other hand, is the progenitor of musicians, flutists and lyre players, though an important horn in Israel was the *shophar*, a ram's horn blown most notably at the New Year ritual. But then things seem to become unusual. Zillah produces Tūbal-Qayin, part of whose name we have seen before in his great-great-great grandfather. The Tūbal part, however, is etymologically related to Yabal

and Yūbal, all derived from a root word having to do with gifts and sacrifices. Yabal's name is related to an animal often sacrificed by Israelites,
and Yūbal's descendants suggest people who participated musically in
religious rituals of various kinds. Tūbal-Qayin's activity for a livelihood
seems curiously double. He is described as "sharpener" of something
made of copper or iron. But the something has so many rather different
meanings that it is very difficult to make out, and its form is that of a
noun meaning someone who does something. That form is done with
the vowels, and we know that sometimes copyists misjudged those. But
its possible underlying meanings range from working crafts with those
metals, to silence or even deafness, and to some sort of magic. I am not
inclined to underestimate the knowledge that ancient Israelites had of
their own language. The meaning of "craftsman" seems the most obvious, but sometimes the most obvious is not necessarily the best. In the
days when these stories were circulating, many people may have seen
the metal trades as some sort of magical activity, and those trades were
relatively recent at that time. The Iron Age in the Near East began about
1400 B.C.E. I'm sorry to confuse the issue, but I can't in good conscience
pretend to know the best answer to it.

Then we have Lemekh's poetic boast to his wives, all unprepared
and without context, except from Qayin. This is a rather ordinary poem
as poetic style goes. It consists of six lines in three parallel pairs. Every
second line in effect repeats, but in slightly different words, what the
first line said. Lemekh has killed somebody—and the style of the poem
is such that "man" and "boy" in verse 23 are very likely to be thought
of as the same person. The bruising that the "boy" has done, however,
might be connected to a verb that sometimes refers to magical activity,
charming, or conjuring. You begin, perhaps, to understand the difficulty
a translator sometimes has in making sense of what is before the eyes
and deciding on a single, creditable solution to its complications. We
translators often wish that the etiquette of translation would allow pro-
viding several alternatives along with the one word we decide to choose.
That is the advantage of being able to expand interpretively to pursue
the alternatives, whether with notes or with essays like these. On the

other hand, translations made by committees, the fate of most biblical translations, often go for the easiest solution. Committees tend not to like, and therefore simply rule out, double or uncertain but possible meanings. This entire passage seems to contain more magic under the surface than one might expect. The number seven was also in the ancient world a magical number and not necessarily a positive one. Killing Qayin would bring the threat of sevenfold punishment. Lemekh multiplies the magical threat for a lesser crime beyond any reason.

Adam gets back to his progenitor's work, with another son. Notice that Chavah does the naming, which was not surprising in Israel. And as is so frequent, the name, Shet (in English, Seth), is explained by a pun—the verb "has given" in verse 25 being *shat* (pronounced approximately like "shot"). Shet does his own naming of his own son, who is 'Enōsh, the meaning of which is closely related to "man." (A brief linguistic detour: the plural of *'iš*, the word for "man" in 2.23, is *'ᵉnašîm*, so perhaps you can see where 'Enōsh came from. It is one of many words in many languages that have mixed backgrounds—think of English "I go" but in the past tense "I went," derived from a different verb.) Our English names come from so many differing linguistic sources that we often have no idea what a personal name might mean. I myself found out at about age twenty-five the Anglo-Saxon meaning of my first name. All Hebrew names mean something in the language, and 'Enōsh, derived from *'iš*, is not a variant of Adam, which means more generally "human."

Finally we have a footnote on religious history: "Then was begun invoking the name of Yahweh." We have seen that name before, but mostly in narration and seldom in the mouth of any character. When Chavah and the snake talked, it was of Elohîm, and she refers again in 4.25 to Elohîm.[b] And in the chapter to follow it is all Elohîm. To be sure, Chavah did say of the birth of Qayin, "I have 'gotten' a man with Yahweh" (4.1), whatever that means. A clear statement suggesting the first presentation of that name to Israelites is given in Exodus 3.15 in a command to Moses backed up by the name Yahweh. That passage, set beside this one, suggests that there were at least two strands of Israelite thought about the use of the divine name Yahweh, one of which traced the use of the name to Moses and the Exodus. But clearly the remark in Genesis points to another strand that traced the name to the tradition's earliest times. Again it is not only interesting but praiseworthy that the tradition maintained intact some of these variations and differences.

We continue with a rather lengthy genealogy, which may be more detailed than you would like, and if you wish, you may skip it. There are some interesting things in it, which you might prefer not to miss.

CHAPTER 6

SOME MORE DESCENDANTS

5 ¹This is the book of Adam's generations. On the day when Elohîm created Adam, he made him in his likeness. ²Male and female he created them, and he blessed them and called their name Adam in the day he created them.ᵃ ³And Adam lived 130 years and he sired in his likeness, according to his image, and he called his name Shet. ⁴After he sired Shet, Adam's days were 800 years, and he sired sons and daughters. ⁵And all Adam's days that he lived were 930 years, and he died.

⁶And Shet lived 105 years and sired ʾEnōsh. ⁷And Shet lived after siring ʾEnōsh 807 years, and sired sons and daughters. ⁸And all of Shet's days were 912 years, and he died.

⁹And ʾEnōsh lived 90 years and sired Qēnan. ¹⁰And after he sired Qēnan ʾEnōsh lived 815 years and sired sons and daughters. ¹¹And all of ʾEnōsh's days were 905 years, and he died.

¹²And Qēnan lived 70 years and sired Mahᵃlalʾel. ¹³And after he sired Mahᵃlalʾel Qēnan lived 840 years and sired sons and daughters. ¹⁴And all of Qēnan's days were 910 years, and he died.

¹⁵And Mahᵃlalʾel lived 65 years and sired Yered. ¹⁶And after he sired Yered Mahᵃlalʾel lived 830 years and sired sons and daughters. ¹⁷And all of Mahᵃlalʾel's days were 895 years, and he died.

¹⁸And Yered lived 162 years and sired Chᵃnōkh. ¹⁹And after he sired Chᵃnōkh Yered lived 800 years and sired sons and daughters. ²⁰And all of Yered's days were 962 years, and he died. ²¹And Chᵃnōkh lived 65 years and sired Mᵉtūshelach. ²²And Chanōkh walked with the Elohîm after he sired Mᵉtūshelach 300 years and sired sons and daughters. ²³And all of Chᵃnōkh's days were 365 years. ²⁴And Chᵃnōkh walked with the Elohîm, and he wasn't there because Elohîm took him.

²⁵And Mᵉtūshelach lived 187 years and sired Lemekh. ²⁶And after he sired Lemekh Mᵉtūshelach lived 782 years and sired sons and daughters. ²⁷And all of Mᵉtūshelach's days were 969 years, and he died.

²⁸And Lemekh lived 182 years and sired a son. ²⁹And he named him Nōach, saying, "This one will 'comfort' us from our toil and our hands' pain from the ground which Yahweh cursed." ³⁰And Lemekh lived after he sired Nōach 595 years and sired sons and daughters. ³¹And all of Lemekh's days were 777 years, and he died.

³²And Nōach was 500 years old, and Nōach sired Shem, Cham, and Yephet.

As you can see from this chapter, someone decided exactly how to write up a genealogy. It's not the way we do it nowadays, but it is certainly clear, concise, and consistent, even if not complete. Except for a few interpolated, extra comments, it's always the same: "And X lived Y years and sired Z. And after he sired Z, he lived A years and sired sons and daughters. And all of X's days were B years, and he died." We are to be interested only in the men of the generations, and in the first son of each man in the genealogy, until the last one. We are not to care about the names of wives or the identities of other children of the figures in the list. In Israel, the eldest son was the inheritor of whatever wealth and property his father left.

And, of course, there are those numbers of years. Did their authors expect their readers to believe them? Or did Sportin' Life have the right biblical commentary in George Gershwin's opera, *Porgy and Bess*, in the song "It ain't necessarily so"? "But no gal will give in / to no man who's livin' / 969 years." Probably the authors believed the numbers. Many cultures, including the early cultures of Mesopotamia, assumed that the old fellows in the earliest times in human history lived prodigiously long lives. The Sumerian king list, which purports to record the reigns of Sumerian kings from the time kingship began, gives numbers for the ancient kings that make the Hebrew patriarchs look positively infantile. It begins with two kings of the city of Eridu who reigned respectively 28,800 and 36,000 years (the Sumerian years were about as long as ours). The numbers tend to diminish as time goes on. After Gilgamesh—a famous Sumerian and later Babylonian hero and the center of the world's earliest epic poem—who reigned for only 126 years, his successors in the city of Uruk ruled normal lengths of time. The longest Sumerian reigns were before the Flood, a story that the Mesopotamians shared with—probably bequeathed to—the Hebrews. Some people who want to think that the Bible never made a mistake wish to suppose that in ancient times, years were much shorter than they are now. There is nothing to indicate that at all. As a matter of fact, the Israelite year was slightly shorter than ours, twelve months of 30 days each, hence 360 days, so that they needed to add a thirteenth month at appropriate times in order to keep sunrise and sunset at the right times. And that matter is complicated by the fact that the lunar calendar of months 29½ days long was also used to establish dates. Such facts do not easily make sense of a life 969 years long.

We begin with a précis of the creation of the humans in the same language as in chapter 1. A curious thing is said in verse 2 about the male and female humans' being created: Elohîm "called their name Adam." It applies the name Adam to both people. The Hebrew word *'adam*, as I noted in discussing chapter 1, means "human"; indeed its general meaning is "humanity," the whole race. So this simply applies the name, earlier applied to the man alone, to both. We have seen that the word for a male human is *'îš*, and for a female human we have the feminine form, *'iššah*.

As the genealogy proper begins, with the earliest generation after the death of Hebel and the banishment of Qayin, there has clearly been a little copying error somewhere along the line. Verse 3, after noting Adam's 130 years, refers to his siring, but does not say that it is a son, just that he sired "in his likeness, according to his image," and gives the name. I think we may presume that the text after "he sired" originally said "a son." But it

doesn't now, and I refuse to insert the word presumptuously. You may notice first that Adam's siring is like Elohîm's creating of the humans, in 1.26,
"in his image and according to his likeness." So there is something about
human fatherhood that is at least analogous to divine creation. To be sure,
we think of our children as like us, sometimes frighteningly so, both in
looks and in personal characteristics. Whether Genesis 1 is the origin of
the metaphor of Father for the deity is in my view uncertain, but it may
be part of it. And the whole idea of humans being in the image of Elohîm
in chapter 1 is less than absolutely clear. You may also notice that here
Adam names Shet, whereas in the account of Shet's birth in 4.25, Chavah
names him. But there are no wives in chapter 5, except in the obvious implication that they were necessary participants in the procreations.

There are some connections between this list and the list of Qayin's
descendants in chapter 4, and also some inconsistencies between the
lists. Side-by-side lists may be enough to show what we need. I have arranged them to show some correspondences, but each list is in its own
proper order.

4.17ff	5.1ff
	Adam
	Shet
	ᵉEnōsh
Qayin	Qēnan
Chᵃnōkh	Mahᵃlal'el
ʿÎrad	Yered
Mᵉhūya'el	Chᵃnōkh
Mᵉtūsha'el	Mᵉtūshelach
Lemekh	Lemekh
Yabal, Yūbal, Tūbal-Qayin	Nōach

The first three in chapter 5 are also named at the end of chapter 4.
But in chapter 5, Qēnan is surely a variant of Qayin, Mahᵃlal'el of
Mᵉhūya'el, Yered of ʿÎrad, Mᵉtūshelach of Mᵉtūsha'el. Lemekh is the
same in both. Might the tradition have wanted somehow to separate
Adam from responsibility for Qayin? It could not very well have done

so, given the detailed story in chapter 4, and the storytellers ended up being true to both sides of the tradition. There are differences of order, such as the fact that in chapter 4, 'Îrad is the son of Chᵃnōkh, but in chapter 5, Chᵃnōkh is the son of Yered. These are just the sorts of differences we might expect if the genealogies had been passed down among different groups as oral tradition for centuries. Notice, too, that the whole group in chapter 4 are descendants of Qayin, and that list ends with Lemekh's boast about Qayin's being avenged, whereas in chapter 5 their counterparts are immediate descendants of Adam. That too might explain the differences. Someone might not have wanted the names to be exactly alike, and a few similarities would not be worrisome. I incline to think that the two lists came down by memory through different channels, and the people responsible for putting them next to each other didn't want to omit anything that might be true. This kind of lore, the sort that is expected to be memorized by people who care about it, tends to be quite stable, perhaps unlike the stories, which might have been known in general terms by the storytellers, who probably would have done some improvising of language and event as they told the tales to audiences. And audiences might have been familiar with tales in general, knowing the episodes that were to be expected but not necessarily the very words in which they would be told.

Then there is the somewhat mysterious remark about Chᵃnōkh, who walked with Elohîm. The second time that is said, the text has a definite article with the word Elohîm: "Chᵃnōkh walked with the Elohîm." I had reason to note with chapter 1 that this term for the deity is plural in form. Why the definite article is here is uncertain, though it might suggest that he walked with multiple Elohîm. What the walking means is also debatable; it may imply both a close friendship and something of a nomadic life. Chᵃnōkh lives the shortest life of all of these folks, a "mere" 365 years. But suddenly, after 365 years, he disappears. There is no language about a death. "He wasn't there" or, perhaps, translating more literally, "There was none of him," "because Elohîm took him." Took him how and where? We don't know. It is most unusual in this book. Not everyone in the Bible is a symbol or example of something, and Chᵃnōkh is like that. He simply disappears, and that may partially explain why his name was applied as the source in some much later Jewish books. There are at least two books of "Enoch," containing some very wild and awfully interesting speculations about heaven and such places and predictions of coming cosmic events. The use of his name for such speculations no doubt derived from this report of his having so mysteriously disappeared by the agency of Elohîm. Anyone who "walked with the Elohîm" and whom Elohîm "took" must have had remarkable knowledge and capabilities.

And then we get to Lemekh's son Nōach. It's too bad that English lacks letters for some Hebrew sounds. We are so used to *Noah*, because English cannot handle the very strong consonant at the end of his He-brew name. I have transcribed it as *ch*, and it should sound like the *ch* in the German name Bach. *Nōach* is more of a mouthful than *Noah* (apologies to readers named Noah—maybe you'd like to change it). But Nōach, alone of all the people so laboriously listed in the genealogy, has a sententious pun on his name. "This one will comfort us" (*nacham*). The verb in the pun is not related to Nōach's name, which is derived from a verb that means to settle down, even to rest (but not the one that explained the Sabbath). The storytellers were probably satisfied to have a word with a sound similar to the name. Maybe comfort from the pain of toil on the ground, the curse on Adam, was more important to them than accurate etymology. But the interesting thing about the explanation is that, in a passage that names Elohîm a good many times and Yahweh only in this sentence, the curse of the ground is said to have come from Yahweh. Was Yahweh felt to be a specialist in curses?

Finally, the last sentence of the passage points forward. That seems to be a stylistic mark of these stories. They often end with statements that have more to do with what follows than with what went before. Here we have reference to the births of Nōach's three sons, Shem, Cham, and Yephet, who will figure prominently later in and after the Flood story.

But first there is a curious, sexy little tale that has bothered people quite a lot.

CHAPTER 7

UNUSUAL BIRTHS

6 ¹And it happened, when the humansª began to multiply on the ground, and daughters were born to them, ²that the sons of the Elohîm saw the daughters of the humans, that they were beautiful, and they took for themselves wives from all that they chose. ³And Yahweh said, "My breath will not . . .ᵇ among the humans permanently; by mistake they are flesh. But their days shall be 120 years." ⁴The Nᵉphîlîm were on Earth in those days, and also afterwards whenᶜ the sons of the Elohîm came to the daughters of humans, who gave birth to them. These were the heroes who were age-old, renowned men.

It's not a story that releases its meaning easily, and there are some difficulties in the text itself. The main one is the word in verse 3 that I have left untranslated. It is a verb that appears nowhere else in the Hebrew Bible, and its meaning is not known. Dictionaries tend to say things like "context suggests 'remain'," and it does, but I would rather leave a gap. In the same sentence, I have translated a somewhat obscure form of what looks like a verb meaning "to sin, to make an error" as "by mistake." I am not totally convinced of that meaning, but the whole sentence is very obscure indeed. If we take it as it looks, it seems like another one of those things that have gone wrong with the creation. "By mistake," perhaps, humans "are flesh." What else might they have been? And who made them like that? We must not rest too much weight on this, but we keep coming across bits of what looks like improvising.

The crucial point is those "sons of the Elohîm," who find the "daughters of humans" cute enough to snap them up as wives. Who are those fellows? Well, they are pretty unquestionably divine male beings, and the phrase suggests the translation "sons of the gods." Some folks who insist that there can be no such things will call them "angels," which strikes me as a theologically driven cop-out. The Hebrew language sometimes uses the phrase "son(s) of" to mean persons or beings belonging to the category of which they are "sons." A "son of the East," for instance, a description of Job in his book, certainly means something like "an easterner." The assumption in this story seems to be that divine beings and human ones could interbreed, an idea the Greeks freely entertained. What are they doing in a monotheistic book? Well, they are marrying human women, that's what, and that suggests once again that the book may not be as monotheistic as we have been taught. This is not the only place in the Hebrew Bible that such beings turn up. In the first two chapters of Job there are gatherings of "sons of Elohîm" with Yahweh, where an argument about Job takes place between Yahweh and a character who has usually been called Satan, but who clearly belongs among the "sons of Elohîm"—and who, I believe, belongs there as a kind of divine District Attorney. In my book on Job I call him "the Prosecutor."[d] Like the snake in the garden, he is almost certainly not a devil. And there are suggestions of a divine court elsewhere, in Elohîm's remark, "Let us make humans in our image" (1.26), and in the meeting mentioned in 3.22. The subsequent introduction of characters called "angels," which in Hebrew, and also in the Greek word behind "angel," means "messenger," does not seem to explain adequately the "sons of the Elohîm."

All of this leads to a conclusion on Yahweh's part that human life must be given a boundary. Surely it has had some sort of boundary since the Adam were sent out of Eden, but the boundary was fairly liberal if Mᵉtūshelach's 969 years is any indication. (However, if you carefully add up the years, you will discover that Mᵉtūshelach died in the Flood, and the text makes it clear what sort of people died in the Flood.) One hundred and twenty years is the divine verdict, but even at the end of chapter 11 we will see ages considerably beyond that. Abraham, whom we meet at the very end of chapter 11, lived 170 years (Gen. 25.7); Isaac, 180 (35.28); and Jacob, 147 (47.28). So the 120-year limit may be for more or less ordinary folks, but not for the great ones of the tradition—though Moses, surely one of the great ones, lived just 120 years (Deut. 34.7), perhaps to make sure he was within the limits. Again, we are doubtless seeing the presence of that assumption that the really great ancient ancestors lived very long lives.

And these ancestors are assumed to be great, as the text calls them the "age-old heroes" and the "renowned men"—the phrase translates a Hebrew phrase that means "men of name." There is, however, a curious name that the text gives them. They were the Nᵉphîlîm. The etymological base of *nᵉphîlîm* is a verb meaning "to fall." I'm not sure how seriously to take that or what shade of its possible meanings to attach to the word. Perhaps there was once a story behind it, or even a joke. On the other hand, the Nᵉphîlîm turn up elsewhere, in Numbers 13.33, in a frightening report from some scouts sent by Moses into southern Canaan, the territory to which the Israelites were returning after the Exodus from Egypt. They report the Nᵉphîlîm as gigantic people ("we looked to them like grasshoppers," they say), with the result that no one wants to go into Canaan right there. That is doubtless why, in Genesis 6.4, the King James version translated "there were giants in the earth in those days," which may remind you, if you're old enough, of a novel titled *Giants in the Earth*, which I read in high school. This tale may have given rise to Milton's portrayal of fallen angels in *Paradise Lost*—he did know Hebrew. But if the story involves a joke, it may slyly suggest that "renown" and the status of "hero" are not unambiguously positive.

We keep coming across ways in which the creation was not working out the way the creator intended, necessitating new responses and requirements and setting more rigorous boundaries. And we are not finished with that, as the sequel shows.

CHAPTER 8

THE FLOOD(S)

In the Flood, we meet a new method of storytelling. The creation presented two quite different tales set down one after the other. The Flood story weaves together two almost entire and different stories, with distinguishable parts following on one another. It's almost as if members of a family were sitting around recalling the same event somewhat differently, and interrupting each other with "No, it wasn't like that, it was like this." Yet the two stories work together remarkably well.

Some distinguishing marks differentiate the two stories. One story—we'll call it Flood 1—characteristically refers to the deity as Yahweh, has seven pairs of "clean" animals and birds and one pair of "unclean" animals brought into the ship (I'll discuss "clean" and "unclean" later), and has a rainstorm lasting forty days. The other story—Flood 2—refers to the deity as Elohîm, narrates Nōach's building of his vessel (a detail not present in Flood 1), has only one pair of all the animals, and its flood involves those cosmic waters we saw in chapter 1 and lasts 150 days, with another 150 days (five months) before the land is dry. Flood 1, probably the earlier of the two, has a style similar to that of the second creation story, such as using the name Yahweh. Flood 2's style is very like that of the first creation story, uses Elohîm, and its tendency to repeat phrases sometimes gets a bit wearisome.

These stylistic similarities from one episode to another have been part of the proposal that the first five books of the Hebrew Bible were put together by combining over a period of time four or more separate written documents into one. The Jewish tradition has called these the "Five Books of Moses," with the assumption that Moses wrote them, and the five, Genesis, Exodus, Leviticus, Numbers, and Deuteronomy, are generally called the Pentateuch, which means "five books." This scholarly hypothesis about the composition of the five books finds throughout them continuing use of such styles as we see in the two creation stories and in the interwoven stories of the Flood. (A slightly longer but, I hope, not too complicated account of this hypothesis of the composition of the Pentateuch is in Chapter Eleven, note e.) I am not convinced that the matter should be taken to the point of overall written documents, but it takes a lot of mental twisting and turning to refuse perceiving the Flood story as the interweaving of two distinct accounts. We should, indeed, be grateful to the ancient editors for keeping elements of both stories. And I will want to introduce some details from the even older Mesopotamian flood stories to suggest that this was a long-lasting tale that caught the imaginations of several cultures—and there are stories of large floods in other cultures as well.

In the translation, the text of Flood 1 is in ordinary roman type, and that of Flood 2 is in *italic* type. For short intrusions of one story into the other I will follow that same scheme, as in the latter part of 8.2.

Flood 1

6   [5]And Yahweh saw that the evil of the humans[a] in Earth was great, and that every inclination of his heart was only evil all the time. [6]And Yahweh regretted that he had made humans on Earth, and he was grieved in his heart. [7]And Yahweh said, "I will wipe out the humans I created from the surface of the ground, from human to cattle, to creepers, and to birds of Sky. For I'm sorry I made them."

[8]But Nōach found favor in Yahweh's eyes.

Flood 2

⁹ *These are Nōach's generations: Nōach was a righteous man, moral in his generations. Nōach walked with the Elohîm.* ¹⁰*And Nōach sired three sons, Shem and Cham and Yephet.*

¹¹*And Earth was spoiled before Elohîm, and Earth was full of violence.* ¹²*And Elohîm saw Earth, and there! it was spoiled. For all flesh spoiled its path on Earth.*

¹³*And Elohîm said to Nōach, "An end of all flesh has come before me, for Earth is full of violence before them. And I will despoil them with Earth.* ¹⁴*Make yourself a ship of gopher wood; you shall make compartments for the ship, and you shall cover it inside and outside with pitch.* ¹⁵*And this is how you shall make it:* 300 *cubits the ship's length,* 50 *cubits its width,* 30 *cubits its height.*ᵇ ¹⁶*A roof you shall make for the ship and finish it to a cubit from the top, and you shall put the ship's door in the side. You shall make it with a bottom, a second, and a third deck.* ¹⁷*And I, look here! will bring the flood of water on Earth to spoil all flesh in which is the breath of life from beneath Sky. Everything in Earth will perish.* ¹⁸*And I have established my covenant with you, and you will come into the ship, you and your sons and your wife and your sons' wives with you.* ¹⁹*And from everything living, from all flesh, two from each you shall bring with you to the ship to keep them alive with you; they shall be male and female.* ²⁰*From the birds by their kinds, and from the cattle by their kinds, and from all the creepers on the ground by their kinds, two from each shall come to you to keep them alive.* ²¹*And as for you, take some of all the food that is to be eaten and gather it to yourself, and it will be food for you and for them."* ²²*And Nōach did according to everything that Elohîm had commanded him, so he did it.*

7 ¹And Yahweh said to Nōach, "Come, you and all your household, to the ship,

for I have seen that you are righteous in this generation.

²From all the clean animals take with you seven pairs, male and mate; and from the animals that are not clean two, male and mate. ³Also from the birds of Sky seven pairs, male and female, to keep alive descendants on Earth. ⁴For seven days from now I will bring rain on Earth

for forty days and forty nights and I will wipe out from the ground's surface everything standing that I made." ⁵And Nōach did everything as Yahweh commanded him.

⁶*And Nōach was six hundred years old when the flood happened, water on Earth.* ⁷*And Nōach and his sons and his wife and his sons' wives with them went into the ship away from the flood waters.* ⁸*Of the clean animals and the animals that were not clean and the birds and all the creepers on the ground,* ⁹*two by two came to Nōach to the ship, male and female, as Elohîm had commanded Nōach.* ¹⁰*And the seventh day came, and the flood waters came on Earth.* ¹¹*In the six-hundredth year of Nōach's life, in the second month on the seventeenth day of the month, on that very day*

> *the fountains of the great Thᵉhōm burst*
> *and the windows of Sky were opened*

¹²And rain came on Earth forty days and forty nights.

¹³*On that very day, came Nōach and Shem and Cham and Yephet, Nōach's sons, and his wife and his sons' three wives with them into the ship.* ¹⁴*They and all the beasts by their kinds, and all the cattle by their kinds, and all the creepers that creep on Earth by their kinds, and all the birds by their kinds, every winged bird.* ¹⁵*And they came to Nōach to the ship, two by two from all the flesh in which is the breath of life.* ¹⁶*And those who came, male and female of all flesh, came as Elohîm had commanded Nōach.*

And Yahweh shut him in. ¹⁷And the flood was on Earth for forty days, and the water increased and lifted the ship, and it rose above Earth.

¹⁸*And the water swelled and increased over Earth, and the ship rode on the water.* ¹⁹*And the water increased more and more over Earth, and it covered all the high mountains that were under all of Sky.* ²⁰*Fifteen cubits the water increased and it covered the mountains.* ²¹*And all flesh that creeps on Earth died, with birds and cattle and beasts, and all the swarming things that swarm on Earth, and all the humans,* ²²*everything in whose nostrils is the breath of life that was on dry land died.* ²³*And it wiped out everything that existed on the ground, from human to cattle, to creepers, and to birds of Sky, and they were wiped out from Earth, and only Nōach and those with him in the ship were left.* ²⁴*And the water increased over Earth for 150 days.*

8   ¹*And Elohîm remembered Nōach and all the beasts and all the cattle that were with him in the ship. And Elohîm made a wind blow over Earth, and the water went down.* ²*And the fountains of Tehōm and the windows of Sky were stopped up,*

and the rain from Sky came to an end.

³*And the water continually receded and went down from the end of* 150 *days.* ⁴*And the ship came to rest in the seventh month, on the seventeenth day of the month, on the mountains of Ararat.* ⁵*And the water continually went down until the tenth month; in the tenth, on the first of the month, the peaks of the mountains could be seen.*

⁶At the end of forty days, Nōach opened the window of the ship that he had made. ⁷And he sent out the raven, which went out and back until the water had dried from Earth. ⁸Then he sent out the dove to see whether the water had decreased from the ground. ⁹But she did not find a place to set her foot, and she returned to him to the ship, for the water was still all over Earth. And he put out his hand and took her and brought her to him into the ship. ¹⁰And he waited yet another seven days and again sent out the dove from the ship. ¹¹And the dove came back at evening, and there in her bill was a plucked olive leaf, and Nōach knew that the water had diminished from Earth. ¹²And he waited still another seven days and sent out the dove, and she did not return to him again.

¹³*In the 601st year, on the first day of the first month, the water dried from Earth, and Nōach removed the cover from the ship, and he looked and, there, the water had dried from the ground's surface.* ¹⁴*In the second month, the twenty-seventh day of the month, Earth was dry.*

¹⁵*Elohîm spoke to Nōach, saying,* ¹⁶*"Go out of the ship, you and your wife and your sons and your sons' wives with you.* ¹⁷*Bring out with you all the beasts who were with you from all flesh, birds, cattle, and all the creepers that creep on Earth, and they will swarm on Earth and be fruitful and multiply on Earth."* ¹⁸*And Nōach went out, and his sons and his wife and his sons' wives with him.* ¹⁹*All the beasts, all the creepers and all the birds, everything that creeps on Earth by their families came out from the ship.*

²⁰And Nōach built an altar to Yahweh, and he took from all the clean animals and from all the clean birds, and he made burnt offerings

on the altar. ²¹And Yahweh smelled the sweet smell, and Yahweh said to himself, "I will not ever curse the ground again because of humans, though the devices of humans' heart are evil from his youth, and I will never again destroy all the living, as I have done.

²²While Earth lasts,
seed and harvest,
cold and heat,
summer and winter,
day and night
shall not stop."

9   ¹*And Elohîm blessed Nōach and his sons, and he said to them, "Be fruitful and multiply and fill Earth. ²And the fear and dread of you shall be upon all of Earth's beasts and upon all of Sky's birds, upon all that creep the ground and upon all Sea's fishes; into your hand they are given. ³Every creeper that is alive is food for you. Like the green plants, I gave you all of them. ⁴Only you are not to eat flesh with its life force, its blood. ⁵But for your blood of your life forces I will make a demand, from the hand of every beast I will demand it; and at the hand of men, at the hand of a man, his brother, I will demand human life.*

⁶*Who sheds the blood of man,*
by man his blood will be shed.
For in the image of Elohîm
he made humans.
⁷*And you, be fruitful and multiply,*
swarm on Earth
and multiply in it."

⁸*And Elohîm said to Nōach and his sons with him, saying, ⁹"And as for me, now I raise my covenant with you and with your descendants after you, ¹⁰and with all the living things that are with you, with birds and with cattle and with all the animals of Earth with you, from all who came out of the ship to all the animals of Earth. ¹¹I have raised my covenant with you, and never again will all flesh be cut off by the floodwater, and there*

will not again be a flood to destroy Earth." ¹²And Elohîm said, "This is the covenant that I make between me and you and all living beings with you for permanent generations. ¹³I have put my bow in the cloud, and it will be a sign of the covenant between me and Earth. ¹⁴And it will be, when I bring clouds over Earth, and the bow is visible in Earth, ¹⁵then I will remember my covenant between me and you and all living beings among all flesh. And there will not again be the floodwater to destroy all flesh. ¹⁶And when the bow is in the clouds, then I will see it to remember the permanent covenant between Elohîm and all the living beings among all flesh that is on Earth." ¹⁷And Elohîm said to Nōach, "This is the sign of the covenant that I have raised between me and all flesh that is on Earth."

Well, things have gone catastrophically wrong. Somehow the creator's shiny new world has been defaced, and the creator had no contingency plans in place and made some doubtful decisions. Maybe we should have noticed more carefully that first misstep, when in chapter 2 Yahweh decided that human loneliness was not good and that making animals might solve it. Making animals did not solve it, and the second plan, the making of the woman, alleviated the loneliness but moved on to the conversation with the snake, which ended in the exclusion of the humans from Eden in order to prevent their access to the tree of life. Or perhaps the first misstep was that earlier, unexplained prohibition of eating from the tree of knowledge and the threat of immediate death.

Then Yahweh made things worse, it seems, by refusing without explanation the offering to him made by Qayin, which led to the first human death and the exile of the miscreant. And those "sons of the Elohîm," which we saw reason to think were themselves divine, got themselves entangled with human women, with the apparent result of some rather significant swelling of the collective human ego. Could Elohîm not keep his own kids under control? The snake's promise, that the humans would be "like Elohîm" if they ate the fruit of the tree of knowledge, has brought the world to a point where humans must be eliminated, because they have not only gotten out of hand, they have gone in the wrong direction with their knowledge of good and evil. The storytellers now think that everything has turned evil. And the remark that Elohîm made back in 3.22, that "the man has become like one of us, knowing good and evil," justifying the exclusion from Eden, now has a somewhat queasy ring to it. Does what has happened since then underscore the ways in which humans—proudly billed in 1.26–27 as "the image of Elohîm" and as the rulers of the entire Earth—have become all too much like Elohîm?

So the deity now feels it necessary to massacre his creation in order to correct its sorry condition. Christianity has always referred to this condition as "the Fall"—into a state of what is theologically called Original Sin—but its theological account of the Fall has concentrated solely on human failings, or has sometimes rung in a supernatural evil force, a Devil, to explain how sin entered the world. But theology has not paid attention to ways in which its sacred book suggests that the creator failed the creation, especially by not considering implications of some of his own decisions. Several divine actions seem, on contemplation, to have been less than adequate. The first creation story kept assuring us, day after day, that the work was good, and at the end of the process, in divine perception, even that it was all "very good" (1.31). But in 6.7, Yahweh is said to have "regretted" that he made the humans, and is quoted to the same effect in 6.8: "I'm sorry I made them." This seems more than a bit lame, especially when we see that the decision for destruction includes the animals, who are not singled out as culpable.

As the storytellers very well knew, however, here we are still, with more tales to be told. So the creation was dreadfully damaged, but not obliterated by the creator. The text unfolds in horrifying detail the destruction of what had been presented as the apex of the creation, the human race, with a small fraction exempted and told in advance but the rest left to notice the rising waters too late to do anything about them. Not that anything could be done about them in any case. The animals, with a very few saved out, are also victims of the action, with no slightest indication that anyone, divine or human, thought they were in any sense at fault—only that somewhat odd remark in 6.12 that "all flesh had spoiled its path on Earth." Is that intended to justify the slaughter

of the animals? If so, it fails entirely to explain why the animals deserved
their extinctions. And the massacre comes about not by a god's laying
about him with weapons and roars of rage but at arm's length, by an im-
personal natural force, a rainstorm of forty days and nights or an open-
ing of the sluice gates of cosmic waters for 150 days. But you notice that
the sea creatures were spared all of this. They, of course, could perfectly
happily go on living in the water, though theoretically they might have
been part of that category "all flesh" that had "spoiled its path on Earth."
Of course, the fish were not on Earth but in Sea.

Let us first pay attention to main details of Flood 1, the earlier story,
then to main details of Flood 2, and finally to the way the two have been
woven into what works, even in the face of inconsistencies, as a single
story. For the combination is quite shrewdly accomplished. Hundreds of
very fine readers over many centuries have not noticed the differences,
or have worked harder than they needed to bring them into agreement.

Flood 1 begins with the disastrous shift of the "knowledge of good
and evil" into evil. The human "heart," says the text, has done this. As
the Israelites thought of it, emotions or feeling happened not in the
heart but in the lower intestines, the "bowels." The heart was the locus
of thought, of decision. Thinking, intelligence for them happened not
in the brain, which had no function for them, but in the chest. That
thinking "heart" has turned bad, and that means that the entire mentality, the organ of knowing, has changed. Hence the transformation of
Yahweh's "heart" from something positive to a new understanding and
conclusion, "grievance," a serious change of mind, to regret about his
earlier creative activity. The whole process of creation has turned into
one massive mistake, and it must be undone.

"But Nōach found favor in Yahweh's eyes" (6.7). The next thing
that happens is the Flood 2 account of the building of the ship, which
Flood 1 does not have. I suspect that is not because Flood 1 never had
it, but that the two accounts were so different that they could not very
well be reconciled, and the one in Flood 2 was detailed enough not to
require whatever detail Flood 1 had. That is, of course, pure speculation,
and you are free to disbelieve every word.

When Flood 1 takes up again, Nōach and his family are entering the ship along with the animals. At this point we have a divergence of facts concerning the animals. Flood 1 calls for the animals to be brought in in mated pairs, as does Flood 2, but in Flood 1 there is one pair of what are called "unclean" animals and seven pairs of "clean" animals. The distinction is a ritual one. Israelite ritual law required that animals to be used for sacrifice had to be perfect and unblemished and of certain species. You could sacrifice bovines, for instance, but not pigs. And animals to be used for food (Flood 1 apparently comes from the strand of the story that does not specify at the creation that food for all is vegetarian) had to be of certain kinds. Animals that could not be used for food (and pigs were among them) or for sacrifice were "unclean." There is a convenient, but quite late, listing of the food regulations in Leviticus 11, if you'd like to see what it included in the two categories. This list was probably modified from time to time, and it doubtless shows the culmination of the process, except that the Talmud, that enormous compilation of the debates and regulations by rabbis in post-biblical centuries, has even more detail.

As for the numbers, it seems likely that Flood 1 assumes that when the flood was over, there would need to be sacrifices, which would require certain clean animals, and perhaps it was assumed that the humans would need to eat some meat while the flood was going on. So there would be enough clean animals to meet both needs, as well as the need for at least one pair of each species, clean and unclean, to start the process of restoring the animal population. The one pair of unclean animals was apparently for the latter purpose, as there was no thought that the unclean animals should simply be drowned in the flood. The storytellers did not say why they thought they needed the unclean animals. Perhaps they needed them to maintain the distinction between clean and unclean for Israelite ritual purposes. Or perhaps it was simply that the creation had included them, and they were not guilty as the humans were—even though most of them were slaughtered in the Flood.

This is the forty-day Flood, and it comes about by rain, apparently of the ordinary kind, though forty straight days of rain is to be understood as an enormous, flood-producing downpour. The flood in this version needs to be imagined, as it is not described with anything like the detail of the other story. This one does not indicate anything at all about how deep the water was from forty days of raining. Forty days in Israel was a conventional number for a fairly long time, related also to the forty years that Israel was said to be in the Wilderness after the Exodus and before they returned to Palestine.

In 8.6 the flood is over in this version, and Nōach looks out the ship's open window, and he sends out two birds to scout the terrain. The raven goes out and stays out until everything is dried up. The dove goes out and immediately comes back, not wanting to get its feet wet. So Nōach waits seven days to send the dove out again, and this time it returns with an olive leaf. That is, it seems to me, quite a rapid release of the water, and it may have seemed so to Nōach: he waited another seven days before disembarking.

In the Babylonian flood story, a section of the Epic of Gilgamesh narrated by Utnapishtim, who survived the flood, he also recounts sending out birds, first a dove, which came back, then a swallow, which also came back, both of them because there was still too much water on the ground. Then he sent out a raven, which did not return. This is almost surely a detail that the Israelites got from the Babylonian story and modified in their own way. There is also a Sumerian account of a great flood over the earth, but it does not tell of sending out scouting birds. Both the Sumerian and the Babylonian flood stories describe a flood that lasted only seven days. That may have seemed too few days to the Israelite storytellers, for whom, as I noted above, forty days was a typical longish time. Living in a wide, flat river valley, the Mesopotamians thought that a seven-day downpour was quite enough to send everything over its banks. They knew from floods. The Israelites, living in hilly country sparsely crossed by rivers, were not knowledgeable about floods. Those responsible for the second Hebrew story have an even longer flood, 150 days, which is just five months. Indeed, that one turns into another five months, as it takes a second 150 days for the water to recede. That looks like a detail that dwellers in hilly country would think necessary.

In 8.20 comes the explanation of the different numbers of animals taken into the ship. Nōach builds an altar to Yahweh and makes sacrifices, using clean animals and clean birds. At least one pair of everything had to survive in order to begin the process of renewing the animal and bird populations. It seems probable that the seven pairs of clean animals and birds were more than would be needed for the sacrifices, and perhaps the Israelites also thought it well that the renewed populations of clean beasts should be more numerous than those of the unclean. And, of course, clean ones would have provided some food for the humans during and perhaps immediately after the flood and perhaps also for carnivores among the other animals.

One wonders what it was about animal offerings that was thought to please deities. In the one earlier presence of animal sacrifice, that of Hebel, no mention is made of why Yahweh accepted the sacrifice or what he might have appreciated about it. Apparently the Israelites guessed that the nice smell of the burning was what did it, at least this time. There are indications that some cultures thought that the foods offered in sacrifices actually fed and nourished their deities, but Israel does not seem to have thought of that divine use of sacrifices. In fact, meat from certain sacrifices, described in the later ritual laws, went to the presiding priests, who with their families probably subsisted on such sources of food.

The Israelites decided that Yahweh liked the smell (8.21), and it apparently put him in a good mood in spite of his recollection that humans had been pretty awful. So he decides not ever again to destroy everybody, even though it is not clear that humans have improved at all. At the same time, Nōach has, as the text says, "found favor" with Yahweh, who composes a short poem, promising that the cycles of seasons, temperatures, and day and night will always be in place (8.22). We may well call it a re-creation.

Let us now look more closely at Flood 2, which is quite different. It begins in 6.9–10 with a repetition from the end of chapter 5. And then it goes to one of those almost too typically repetitive passages in verses 11–13, four repetitions of various forms of the same verb, which I have translated "spoil" and, in one case, for a causative form, "despoil." I think we get the picture.

The next activity is to build the ship. I have used that word for it, because as this story describes it, this is a large vessel, 300 cubits long, which comes at the outside to 500 feet. I know it is usually called an ark, and "Noah's Ark" is, of course, perfectly familiar—many of us played with them as children. I suppose the fact that the "ark" is described in Flood 2, which has only one pair of each species of animal, was the reason that the toys always had only one pair of each—of course, it could be expensive to figure out which animals ought to have seven and to provide them. You'd need a bigger toy ark than small children could handle.

The Hebrew word used is somewhat odd for a ship; it was most notably used otherwise in the Bible for the floatable box, certainly not 500 feet long, in which the infant Moses was deposited in the Nile, in Exodus 2 (and perhaps that use of the word was a deliberate echo of the Flood story). But there is not enough description in the text to permit making a sketch of the vessel. It was to be made of "gopher wood," which has nothing to do with the small North American beast of that name. No one knows what kind of wood the Hebrew word *gōpher* designated. Some have speculated from a similarity of letters that it might have been cypress, but I have not wanted to enshrine that guess in our minds. There was a door in the side and apparently a roof of some sort, but the language about finishing it (is that the coat of pitch?) is unclear. And this ship has three decks, no doubt to give enough space for all the people and animals and for the stored food. No sails seem to have been used, and there is no mention of a rudder or other means of steering. The food must last for all the animals and people—this is a much longer flood, as the dates are given in the text, coming to 370 days. It starts on the seventeenth of the second month (7.10), and everything is dry on the twenty-seventh of the next second month (9.14).

As Flood 2 seems to be connected with the first creation story in its style and outlook, we surmise that the story assumes that the food would have been all vegetable. And the fact that this story has only one pair of each species of animals and birds means that the needed store of food was somewhat less per species than in the other story. We will not speculate on the state of the veggies after a year in what could not very well have been cold storage.

Why is there but one pair of all the animals here, as distinguished from the one pair of unclean and seven pairs of clean animals in Flood 1? The story mentions (7.8) both clean and unclean animals but has no difference in their numbers. Nōach makes no sacrifice at the end of this Flood, so there is no need for extra animals to meet that purpose. Moreover, this story is clear that the entire point of bringing animals on board is to preserve all the species for restocking Earth with them when the flood has done its work.

Then the flood comes, and this story is careful to note both Nōach's age—six hundred years—and the date. It is also careful to note, first that the water increased till it covered all the high mountains, and second (7.20), quite strangely, that it rose 15 cubits. That is at best 25 feet, which would not cover even the lowest hills. I wonder if a number somehow dropped out of the text and could never be replaced. Or perhaps it meant, not at all clearly, that the water covered the mountains to the depth of 25 feet.

The mode of the flood is different in this story. "The fountains of the great Tᵉhōm burst." Those are the cosmic waters beneath Earth, sending water up from below. *Thᵉhōm* is the word I translated as "abyss" in 1.2, over which darkness lay before the creation started. It apparently means the cosmic area beneath Earth, and whether its "fountains," which burst open in Flood 2, were thought to be connected to the waters of Sea is uncertain. "And the windows of Sky were opened." That is the cosmic water above what in chapter 1 I called the "bowlshape," the upside-down, solid hemisphere named Sky. It apparently had openings that had previously been closed, and now poured water down from outside Earth. This is not merely rain but something much more serious. It is the undoing of whatever restrained the cosmic waters from the creation, and it is intended to undo the creation itself, so that a new attempt can be made with the tiny remnant of Earth's inhabitants inside that three-decked ship. Unlike Flood 1, there is nothing naturalistic about Flood 2. This is the universe breaking open. It is interesting

that the Babylonian flood story describes the onset of the flood as ter-
rifying the gods as well as massacring the humans.

The water increases for 150 days—five months—and 8.2 appears to
mean that at the end of that time the cosmic sources, the Sky's windows
and the great Tᵉhōm's fountains, were closed. Water no longer came in
to Earth from outside. The text carefully gives the date: the seventeenth
day of the seventh month, precisely five months from the beginning.
That day the ship landed on the top of a mountain somewhere in the
east end of Asia Minor (now Turkey)—and people keep trying to find
its remains on or near Mount Ararat. That they will ever succeed seems
to me not merely doubtful, and what purport to be photographs of it
are clearly fakes.

The ancients cared about the dates, and we will shortly see why.
Two months and thirteen days after the water started receding, the
mountain peaks could be seen. Then we find that the water was dried
on the first day of the first month, the month later known as Nisan.
But that was not New Year's Day in Israel. The new year began on the
first day of the seventh month. It no doubt seems strange to us to have
the new year beginning in the fall—September or October. Europeans
think of winter as the season of death, and spring as the beginning of
new life. In the Near East, summer was the time of death, when the heat
became so intense, and fall was the season when new growth began. So
winter was the season of life in that territory.ᶜ

Now we have the pronouncement of blessing on Nōach and his
sons. We need to keep noticing that the women are not mentioned, nor
is there any reason we should suppose that they were included in the
blessing. They should have been, of course.

Three conditions are laid on the survivors. The first is familiar
from chapter 1: "Be fruitful and multiply and fill Earth" (9.1), though
"subduing" is not included in the imperative, and "multiplying" will
require cooperation from the women. The second has to do with a new
relation to the animals: they are to fear humans, and the humans have
complete control over them (9.2), and are to use them for food (9.3).
At least that seems to be what is said, except that 9.3 refers specifically

to the "creepers," which in chapter 1 seemed to be small beasts like rats and moles and such. Again, might something have been left out of the text? The subsequent law, which this passage seems to know something about, names all sorts of animals that may be sacrificed, and stories tell of various animals that are eaten without any interference from Elohîm. To confine it to the "creepers" seems very odd. But what is clear is that now, unlike in chapter 1, permitted food includes meat, and this passage explicitly states that the meat is like the plants that were previously given for food. Perhaps that is also connected with the fact that the animals are now to fear humans.

That matter demands some comment. Why does Elohîm introduce "fear and dread" into the world? Not that it has been totally absent up to now. But here is the explicit statement that the animals (including the fish) are to fear humans. To be sure, that might be thought to be in some part a safety measure, as animals who do not fear humans will be easy prey when the humans are out looking for dinner. So animal fear may make bagging food a bit harder for the hunters. But "fear and dread" seems a somewhat odd specific quality to be introduced into earthly life immediately after earthly life has been so drastically reduced. To be sure, now that humans are permitted to eat meat—and we may suppose, though it is not stated as such, that animals may now eat each other—a few experiences of being mortally attacked will presumably instill fear into the animal psyche. But why does the text make such a point of the fear in Elohîm's description of the circumstances of life after the Flood? I ask the question because I do not have an answer to it satisfactory to myself.

There is a proviso about this, however: you are not to eat blood, which was thought to be the principal life force. The word that I have translated "life force," *nepheš*, is sometimes translated "soul," but that is a confusion between Hebrew and Greek. Greek knows of a "soul," a *psychē*, but it is a different principle entirely. In Genesis 2, when the man is formed out of dust, and Yahweh breathes breath into his nose, he becomes a "living being," as I translated it there: a *nepheš chayyah*, a somewhat redundant way of saying a *nepheš*, really alive. That expression has traditionally been translated "a living soul." But it's not like the

Greek soul, which was apparently in some respects thought to be indestructible. Part of what is being commanded in 9.4 is not to eat living animals, and that was expanded at some point to require that meat was edible under Jewish law only if the blood had been drained out. That is part of what is meant even today by "kosher" meat.[d] But there is no indication that the animals are expected to observe the kosher regulation.

Elohîm's third requirement is that killing humans requires a corresponding and punishing death. Capital punishment is the third law laid down at the end of the Flood, and the opinions on that range from one extreme to another. I personally find capital punishment objectionable, but this is not the place to argue that. The idea is encapsulated in a poem that, however disagreeable may be its thought, is an interesting example of something the ancient Hebrews did with their poetry quite frequently.

> Who sheds the blood of the man,
> by the man his blood will be shed. (9.6)

Notice the order of words: (a) sheds; (b) blood; (c) man; (c') man; (b') blood; (a') shed. The order of words in the second line is the exact reverse of the first in Hebrew as well, which manages to use only three words in each line. We noted the chiasmus in the poem in 2.23. We have here not only a lovely chiasmus but also a nice play of sound with the syllable *dam* (pronounce it *dahm*, not like the earthwork that holds water back), which goes like this:

> *šōphēkh dam ha'adam*
> *ba'adam dammō yiššaphēkh.*

I am pleased by such evidences of imaginative literary skill. At the same time, the poem justifies killing as a punishment for killing. One must wonder about murders done by Elohîm, as in the destruction in the Flood of all the existing human race except Nōach's immediate family. Is Elohîm—and by extension Yahweh as well—at liberty to kill people? Granted, it was punishment for what was perceived as wrong-doing. And perhaps it tried to limit capital punishment to murder, which not all ancient law codes did. Capital punishment is added for animals that kill humans. And strangely, the storytellers used the same language as in human killings, ascribing them to animals' "hands." We assume that the Israelites knew the differences between human and animal anatomy, but in this instance they seem not to notice.

Now Elohîm goes on to establish a covenant, a kind of treaty, between himself and everybody, human and animal, on Earth. He promises to refrain from destroying the creation again by a flood, and presumably the part of the treaty that humans (and animals?) agree to obey is the command to multiply, to refrain from eating blood, and to do proper justice for murder. Elohîm provides a concrete sign that the treaty is in force: the rainbow in the clouds, which shows that the sun is shining and you're not looking at 150 days of water coming at you from above and below. The interesting detail about this is that the rainbow is put there to be the visible reminder *to Elohîm* of his promise and treaty, to make him remember them. The implication that he might conceivably forget this binding treaty is somewhat strange, but he promises not to. And if we want to be picky about it, he promises not to destroy the creation again *by a flood*, but does not include in the treaty that he will not use any other means. No doubt the Israelites couldn't really think of any other way of destroying the creation, unlike us, who are able to think we might destroy it by doing enough damage to the atmosphere. In any case, the Flood survivors are not required to promise not to destroy the creation. Perhaps if they had been, we might have avoided some of our current depredations—though I am cynical enough about our kind to doubt it. Flood 1, now that we think of it, simply gives a promise not to destroy everything again and doesn't specify any means.

Finally, how do these two rather different stories of the Flood now coalesce into one? Well, the fact is that they don't quite. But they come close enough that only in modern times, since perhaps the eighteenth century, have scholars noticed the inconsistencies. But I think the old editors did an awfully good job of it, especially if we don't require that they did it perfectly.

First, in 6.5–8, we have the Flood 1 account of the problem: the thing has gone all wrong, turned only to evil, and Yahweh regrets it. But

Nōach is his prime good example. That is the cue for Flood 2 to bring up Nōach, his genealogy, and the quality of his goodness, and it gives a slightly different account of the world's badness, using its own kind of language for it. It goes on then to the command to Nōach to build the ship, and the series of dimensions and materials, something that Flood 1 does not have—or if it ever did, it has been supplanted. Elohîm mentions the covenant with Nōach and his family and commands him to bring in a pair of each kind of animals to be saved, along with food (6.13–22).

That moves us back to Flood 1 and the different numbers of animals and the news that it will rain for forty days and nights (7.1–5). After that we go back to Flood 2 (7.6–11) and Nōach's age (ripe and old), and close with the description of the cosmic sources of the flood through the windows of Sky and the fountains of Theḥōm, which will last for 150 days. One sentence of Flood 1 intervenes (7.12) with the forty-day rain repeated. It is not hard to suppose that people simply thought, "Oh, well the cosmic stuff goes on longer, but we begin with forty days of rain." Then in 7.13–16, the actual entry of Nōach and all the others into the ship can be mentioned again (Flood 2 has no compunction whatever at repeating what it has already said), and Flood 2 seems to propose an extraordinarily short time for Nōach and his boys to get all the family along with all the animals herded into the ship: "on that very day" (7.13). It is, of course, clear that the Israelites had no notion of how many different species of animals, birds, and other creatures the world actually contained. After that we go briefly back to Flood 1, where Yahweh shut up Nōach, the flood came for its forty days (7.16–17), and the ship floated away. Flood 2 then describes in more detail the rise of the waters and the covering of the mountains, and comes down to the end of the cosmic deluge, the closing of Sky's windows and the Theḥōm's fountains (7.18–8.2), with a very short interpolation of Flood 1 about the rainstorm ending (8.2b). Flood 2 then continues with the ship coming to rest among the mountains of Ararat (8.3–5).

Now we return to Flood 1 and the episode of sending the birds out, a detail that Flood 2 does not have. When the dove does not return at the end of that episode, we go back to Flood 2 and the departure from the ship, along with Flood 2's dates for the end of all of this (8.13–19). Flood 1 resumes with Nōach's building an altar and making sacrifices to Yahweh, who in response promises never again to "curse the ground" and destroy everything, but to maintain the rounds of activities that Earth requires (8.20–22). Flood 2 then has its version of the promise, the covenant with its attendant new regulations, including permission to eat meat but not blood, and requiring punishment for murder. And it all ends with the lovely image of the rainbow as the visible sign of that covenant (9.1–17).

The story really works quite well, moving sensibly from one episode to another. That there is repetition is not a serious barrier to understanding, partly because Flood 2 itself uses a great deal of repetition. But the editors carefully maintained the main outlines of each story, perhaps preferring not to leave out anything that they considered was essential to the story and, as they saw it, true.

CHAPTER 9

YET ANOTHER CURSE—
AND A BLESSING

9 ¹⁸And Nōach's sons who came out of the ship were Shem, and Cham, and Yephet, and Cham was the father of Kᵉnaʻan. ¹⁹These three were Nōach's sons, and from these the world was dispersed. ²⁰And Nōach started to work the ground, and he planted a vineyard. ²¹And he drank some of the wine and was drunk and was uncovered in his tent. ²²And Cham, the father of Kᵉnaʻan, saw his father's nakedness, and he told his two brothers outside. ²³And Shem and Yephet took the sheet, put it on their two shoulders, and walked backwards, and covered their father's nakedness. Their faces were turned away, and they did not see their father's nakedness. ²⁴Nōach woke up from his wine and he knew what his youngest son had done to him. ²⁵And he said:

> Cursed be Kᵉnaʻan,
> slave of slaves
> let him be to his brothers.

²⁶And he said:

> Blessed be Yahweh,
> Shem's god,

and let Keⁿaʿan be his slave.

²⁷May Elohîm ʿenlargeʾ Yephet,
and may he live in Shem's tents,
and let Keⁿaʿan be his slave.

²⁸Nōach lived after the flood 350 years. ²⁹And all of Nōach's days were 950 years, and he died.

This is a strange little tale, which depends for its sense on some Israelite assumptions about life and society. The premise is that Nōach became a farmer after the flood; "started to work the ground" is an interpretive translation of what is more literally "became a man of the ground." He planted a vineyard. The Israelites knew all about vineyards, because Palestine was good wine country. I sometimes think that if the Israelites had settled in Mesopotamia, where the Babylonians were, and all had happened there as it happened in Palestine, then they would not have known all about vineyards, because the Mesopotamian valley is very good for grains such as wheat and barley, and the Babylonians and Assyrians drank a lot of beer. If Christianity had come into being as an heir of the Jewish tradition in Babylonia, then Jews would drink beer at Passover and Christians would today be drinking beer as their Eucharistic drink.

But Nōach planted a vineyard. Of course, the story does not need to remind Israelite hearers that vines take considerable time to mature, and that Nōach could not have had his binge even within a few weeks of planting his vineyard. But he had it, and there came the problem.

Once again the relation to the soil causes difficulty. Somehow folks don't learn from the past or the stories of the past—that might almost be a statement of the human condition. Some people think that Israel's difficulties were traceable to the fact that they stopped being no-mads, moved into Palestine (Canaan, as this story has it), and became farmers, which doubtless exposed them to the kind of fertility-centered religious thinking entailed in farming and animal husbandry. The in-digenous Canaanites were certainly very well acquainted with fertility gods and goddesses. Well, there may have been many temptations open in the ancient world to "servants of the ground," and we've already seen several. Whether behind any of these stories is the idea that the nomadic way of life might have shielded them from the dangers to living and thinking entailed in settled life in fields and cities, I do not know. The thought is worth having in the mind.

This is the second time that nakedness has cropped up as a difficulty. In the garden of Eden, Adam and Chavah were naked and unashamed of it (2.25). Then, having eaten from the tree of knowledge, they realized their nakedness and became afraid of Yahweh because of it. Their fear led Yahweh to realize they had been eating that fruit, which issued in their exclusion from the garden, and also in Yahweh's clothing them. But Nōach's nakedness is a different matter, the stupor resulting from his having too much good wine (perhaps it was not so good after all). Drunkenness in Israel may have been often enough connected with people's becoming naked that they didn't need to explain it. It's not necessarily a surprising state for a drunk to be in, especially in that hot climate, where clothing needs to be spare enough not to be dreadfully uncomfortable. So there he lies, helpless and unconscious. His son Cham sees him in that state, and we have to imagine the style of his telling his brothers about it. Given how serious the outcome is, he might have giggled and said something like, "Hey, catch the old man in there!" or something equally insensitive. There are narrative evidences that the Israelites were protective of their nudity, and one was not supposed to be seen even by close relatives in that state. At any rate, the care with which Shem and Yephet cover Nōach up in such a way as not actually to see him, walking backwards with the sheet and having their heads turned away, shows that it matters.

Cham was the culprit, and Nōach, waking from his wine, somehow mysteriously knew what Cham had done. The text does not relate how Nōach knew that, but it does say something curiously wrong about Cham: that he was Nōach's "youngest son." In all the lists Cham is listed as the second of the three sons, and that kind of list is understood to be in chronological order unless something else is said. By that evidence, we would have to say that Yephet was the youngest. But the Hebrew is quite clear on its construction: it says "youngest." I simply incline to disbelieve it, but as we have no other documentation—and can't get any—we'll just have to leave it as a strange statement.

But the story is focused on the fact that Cham was the father of Kᶜnaᶜan. We know that name more familiarly as Canaan, the territory in which Israel settled on the Mediterranean coast between the Dead Sea and the Mediterranean. Evidently the Israelites assumed that there had to be an ancestor from whom the name had come, and they attributed his descent to Cham. This also shows up in the ethnographic chapter 10, which lists the descendants of the three sons of Nōach.

The strange thing is that the punishment falls not on the guilty Cham but on his son, Kᶜnaᶜan. Kᶜnaᶜan had done nothing, was not even present in this episode, unless he was secretly peeking in the tent flap. Why does he get the curse? More than one hypothesis might be considered. Think first that Cham, as one of Nōach's three sons, with his wife, was a subject of that "covenant" that Elohîm had made after the Flood, which included the safety of all Nōach's immediate family. That might mean that Cham, having been "sanitized" by the covenant, could not be punished as he deserved. But his guilt remained, and it puts another shadow over the effects of the Flood, which was supposed to erase the guilt of the humans for Earth's bad situation. Is that another instance of a lack of divine foresight, in failing to consider that some beneficiary of the covenant might not be equal to its requirements?

Another hypothesis is that because the Israelites had displaced Canaanites from being the major group in the territory, they therefore felt the need in their traditional stories to indicate why they were successful. Not only had they conquered the local Canaanites, according to the Book of Joshua, but the two groups spoke the same language, although the Israelites were the later comers to the territory. So there was already some need to insist on an Israelite priority there. What better background than Nōach's curse on Kᶜnaᶜan by way of Cham? To be sure, the later story of Abraham explains it differently: Yahweh handed the Canaanite territory over to Abraham and his descendants (Gen. 12.1–9). Here, and as we will see in chapter 10, Kᶜnaᶜan belongs to the descendancy of Cham, whereas Israel comes from Shem. So not only were the Canaanites the displaced persons in the Palestinian territory, but they were thought to be of an inferior descent. One must wonder, though, whether the text of the curse originally used the name of Cham instead of that of Kᵉnaʿan, as the cursed person is to be a "slave of slaves" *to his brothers.* That phrase would surely point to Cham, as Shem and Yephet were the uncles, not the brothers, of Kᵉnaʿan. As it stands, we have to see the curse on Kᵉnaʿan as a piece of Israelite political tinkering with the ancestral tradition. Somehow or other, someone thought that a meaningful move would be to shift the blame from Cham, who had done the deed deserving the curse, to Kᵉnaʿan, whose descendants were present in "Israelite" territory.

So Shem and Yephet come in for congratulations on their behavior with their drunken father. And there is—don't be surprised—a nice, linguistically apt pun in the congratulation to Yephet: *yapht ʾᵉlohîm lᵉyephet,* "May Elohîm 'enlarge' Yephet." It's too bad that puns in one language can seldom be transferred to or reflected in puns in another. But these tendencies to want to make puns on people's names is a somewhat endearing stylistic phenomenon.

Finally, Nōach's life is completed. A small point: the Flood came when Nōach was 600 years old (7.6), but it was not completely finished until he was 601 (8.13). The editors seem not to have remembered that, and Nōach should be credited with 951 years. If these storytellers had not done their job to invite and reward careful observation of what they wrote, I would never have noticed that. My doing so is a compliment to them.

CHAPTER 10

DESCENDANTS AND NATIONS

The material that follows contains a lot of names that will probably
mean very little to the reader. It is an account of the peopling of the
world after the Flood left no humans but Nōach and his immediate
family. To be sure, the peoples listed here—and you should assume
that they were groups, not individuals, with one or two exceptions—
were all to be found within relatively close distances from Israel. There
are no Chinese, Eskimos, or Patagonians. Like their neighbors, the
Israelites had no idea of the size of the world or the varieties of peoples
in it. In their lore, the entire world was populated by the descendants
of three men, Shem, Cham, and Yephet, who were all the descendants
left of one man, Nōach. The three sons of Nōach are associated with
certain geographical areas: the descendants of Yephet are mostly European and inhabitants of Asia Minor, those of Cham northeastern
African and southern and western Arabian for the most part, and
those of Shem partly Mesopotamian and areas close to it. The names
have also been used traditionally for linguistic families, though the
identities are not perfectly aligned. The Yephetites seem mostly to be
Indo-European, when they can be identified; the Chamites have been

identified as a language group, called Hamitic and including Egyptian; and Shemites mostly represent Semitic languages—you can see where the term "Semite" came from. "Semite" is in modern days, of course, properly a linguistic term, not a racial one. As both Arabic and Hebrew are Semitic languages, it is an error to confine anti-Semitism to opposition to Jews.

10 ¹These are the generations of Nōach's sons, Shem, Cham, and Yephet, and sons were born to them after the flood.

²The sons of Yephet: Gōmer, Magōg, Madai, Yavan, Tūbal, Meshech, and Tiras. ³The sons of Gōmer: 'Ashkᵃnaz, Rîphat, and Tōgarmah. ⁴The sons of Yavan: 'ᴇlîshah, Tarshîsh, the Kittîm, and the Dōdanîm. ⁵From these the island peoplesᵃ separated themselves in their lands, each with its language, by their clans in their peoples.

⁶The sons of Cham: Kūsh, Mitsrayim, Pūt, and Kᵉnaʿan. ⁷The sons of Kūsh: Sᵉbaʾ, Chᵃvîlah, Sabtah, Raʿmah, and Sabtᵉkaʾ. And the sons of Raʿmah: Shᵉbaʾ and Dᵉdan.

⁸And Kūsh sired Nimrōd, who became the first mighty man in Earth. ⁹He became a mighty hunter before Yahweh. Hence the saying, "Like Nimrōd, a mighty hunter before Yahweh." ¹⁰The beginning of his kingdom was Babel, also 'Erekh, 'Akkad, and Kalneh in the land of Shinʿar. ¹¹From that land 'Asshur went forth and built Nînᵉvēh and Rechōbōth city and Kalach. ¹²And Resen between Nînᵉvēh and Kalach, that is the big city.

¹³And Mitsrayim sired the Lūdîm, the ʿᴬnamîm, the Lᵉhabîm, the Naphtuchîm, ¹⁴and the Patrusîm, the Kasluchîm, from which the Pᵉlishtîm went out, and the Kaphtōrîm.

¹⁵Kᵉnaʿan sired Tsîdōn, his first-born, Chēt, ¹⁶the Yᵉbusî, the 'ᴇmorî, and the Girgashî, ¹⁷the Chivvî, the ʿArqî, and the Sînî, ¹⁸the 'Arvadî, the Tsᵉmarî, and the Chᵃmatî. And later the clans of the Kᵉnaʿᵃnî were dispersed. ¹⁹The border of the Kᵉnaʿᵃnî went from Tsîdōn to Gerar as far as Gaza, going to Sᵉdōm and ʿᴬmorah, 'Admah and Tsᵉboyim as far as Lashaʿ. ²⁰These are the sons of Cham by their clans and languages, in their lands among their peoples.

²¹To Shem too, the ancestor of all the sons of ʿĒber, and the elder brother of Yephet, was born.ᵇ ²²The sons of Shem were ʿĒlam and ʾAsshūr, ʾArpakhshad, Lūd, and ʾᴬram. ²³The sons of ᴬram: ʿŪts, Chūl, Geter, and Mash. ²⁴ʾArpakhshad sired Shelach, and Shelach sired ʿĒber. ²⁵To ʿĒber was bornᶜ two sons; the name of the first was Peleg because in his time the land was divided,ᵈ and his brother's name was Yoqtan. ²⁶And Yoqtan sired ʾAlmōdad and Sheleph, Chᵃtsarmavet and Yerach, ²⁷Hᵃdōram, ʿŪzal, and Diqlah, ²⁸ʿŌbal, ʾᴬbîmaʾēl, and Shᶜbaʾ, ²⁹ʾŌphîr, Chᵃvîlah, and Yōbab. All these were descendants of Yoqtan. ³⁰And their dwellings were from Mēshaʾ to Saphar,ᵉ the eastern hill country. ³¹These are the sons of Shem by their clans and their languages in their lands and nations.

³²These are the clans of the sons of Nōach by their generations in their nations, and from these the nations separated out in Earth after the flood.

We have had reason to notice before that the knowledge of Earth held by the ancient Israelites was quite limited, confined to areas relatively close by. And the account in this chapter of the populating of Earth after the Flood makes this relative nearness quite clear. Scholars speak of this chapter as "The Table of Nations," and as long as we include smaller groups under the rubric of nations, that is all right. We should not think of these nations as if they were modern nation-states. Many of them come closer to being clans or tribes than nations in any modern sense. That is part of what the text means by attaching them to individual ancestors. And, of course, in this tradition, the ancestors worth mentioning are all male, and everything goes from fathers to sons.

I have puzzled over the best method of identifying these peoples. I will try to indicate what seems to me the best estimate of their identity and where they lived. Some of them are simply not known or cannot be guessed at. It is interesting that while Nōach's three sons are usually listed in the order Shem, Cham, and Yephet, as they are in 10.1, the lists of descendents are given in the opposite order—Yephet, Cham, and Shem—perhaps because Israel was understood to belong to the Shemites, which would make sense of their being mentioned last. Finally, I decided to put them in tabular form (below) and expand on some of their identities in notes.

Yephetites

Listed Name	Possible Recognizable Ancient Name [f]	Location
Gōmer	Cimmerians?	near Black Sea, Asia Minor
Magōg [g]	Scythians?	Asia Minor
Madai	Medes	Iran
Yavan	Ionians [h]	western Asia Minor
Tūbal	Tūbal	Asia Minor
Meshech	Meshech	Asia Minor
Tiras [i]	unknown	unknown
'Ashkᵃnaz	connected with Scythians?	Asia Minor
Tōgarmah	connected with Hittites?	southern Asia Minor
'ᴇlîshah	unknown	island of Cyprus
Tarshîsh [j]	unknown	unknown
Kittîm	Cretans?	island of Crete
Rîphat	unknown	unknown
Dōdanim [k]	unknown	unknown

Chamites

Kūsh [l]	Ethiopians or Kassites	Ethiopia or southeastern Mesopotamia
Mitsrayim [m]	Egyptians	Egypt
Pūt [n]	Pūtians	Libya perhaps
Kᵉnaʿan	Canaanites	Canaan (Palestine)
Chᵃvîlah	none known	unknown
Sᵉbaʾ	Sebaʾ	Arabia?
Sabtah	none known	Arabia?
Raʿmah	none known	Arabia?
Sabtᵉkha	none known	Arabia?
Shᵉbaʾ [o]	Sheba	Arabia
Dᵉdan	none known	Arabia?

Nimrōd[p]	individual	unknown
Babel	Babylonians	southern Mesopotamia
ʾErekh[q]	city	southern Mesopotamia
ʾAkkad	Akkadians	southern Mesopotamia
Kalnēh	city	not known
Shinʿar[r]	territory	southern Mesopotamia
ʾAsshūr[s]	Assyrians	northern Mesopotamia
Nînʿvēh	city, capital of Asshūr	northern Mesopotamia
Rᵉchōbōt-ʿîr[t]	city?	Assyria
Kalah	city	about 20 miles south of Nînʿvēh
Resen	city	unknown
Lūdîm[u]	Lūdîm	north Africa?
ʾᴬnamîm	unknown	unknown
Lᵉhabîm	unknown	unknown
Naphtuchîm	unknown	unknown
Patrusîm	Patrusîm	Upper Egypt
Kasluchîm	unknown	unknown
Pᵉlishtîm[v]	Philistines	seacoast of Canaan
Kaphtōrîm	Cretans[w]	island of Crete

Then there is Kᵉnaʿan, and his descendants are cities and groups in and around Canaan (that is, Palestine)—not surprising, as the Israelites would have been quite familiar with all of these groups. Exactly where some of them lived is not certain. The Canaanite territory is described in the text as extending from Sidon, a coastal city in the north (now in Lebanon), south to Gerar near Gaza (now in the Palestinian-controlled Gaza Strip), and east to Sodom, Gomorrah, Admah, and Zeboyim, which were cities at the very southern end of the Dead Sea, inland from the Mediterranean coast. That description probably intended to include other parts of the territory eastward from the coast, besides the four cities last named. A number of them have the same suffix, -*î*, on their names, a gentilic suffix, which we could render "-ites," as in Canaanites, Israelites, and so on. We use this gentilic even today in referring to inhabitants of Israel as Israeli, or those of Iraq as Iraqi. Several of these groups are said in Joshua 3 to have been displaced by the invading Israelites.

Tsîdōn	Sidon, city	coast in Phoenician area
Chēt[x]	Hittites (but not those in Asia Minor)	Palestine
Yᵉbûsî	Yᵉbûsî	city of Yᵉbūs, later Jerusalem
'ᴇmorî [y]	Amorites	everywhere in Canaan
Girgashî	Girgashites	unknown
Chivvî	Hivites	unknown
ʿArqî	unknown	unknown
Sînî	Sinites	unknown
'Arvadî	Arvadîtes	city in Phoenicia
Tsᵉmarî	unknown	unknown
Chᵃmatî	Hamathites	Syrian city

Shemites

ʿĒlam	Elamites	Mesopotamia, east of Tigris River
'Asshūr[z]	Assryians	northern Mesopotamia
'Arpakhshad	Arpakhshad	unknown, probably Mesopotamia
Lūd[aa]	Lydia?	Asia Minor
'ᴀram[bb]	Aram	modern Syria
ʿŪts[cc]	Uz	probably Arabia
Chūl	unknown	unknown
Geter	unknown	unknown
Mash	unknown	unknown
Shelach	unknown	unknown
ʿĒber[dd]	ʿĒber	unknown
Peleg[ee]	Peleg	Mesopotamia?
Yoqtan	unknown	unknown (Arabia?)
'Almōdad	unknown	unknown (Arabia?)
Sheleph	unknown	unknown (Arabia?)

Chᵃtsarmut	unknown	unknown (Arabia?)
Yerach	unknown	unknown (Arabia?)
Hᵃdōram	unknown	unknown (Arabia?)
'Ūzal	unknown	unknown (Arabia?)
Diqlah	unknown	unknown (Arabia?)
'Ōbal	unknown	unknown (Arabia?)
'ᴬbîma'ēl	unknown	unknown (Arabia?)
Shᵉba'	Sheba	Arabia
'Ōphîr⁽ᶠᶠ⁾	'Ōphîr	Arabia, north Africa?
Chᵃvîlah⁽ᵍᵍ⁾	unknown	unknown
Yōbab	Yōbab	probably Arabia or Edom

Not what you would call the most gripping section of the Hebrew Bible. It is worth repeating that this was lore of a sort unquestionably important to the ancient Israelites, who would have known more about these groups than we can reconstruct from our distance. Had they not felt the importance of such lore, they would not have recorded it in such detail. So we need to be respectful in our ways. They certainly wished to be well informed about all the people who lived within their knowledge, which is more than some ancient (or some modern) peoples cared about. But I suggest that we need not spend a lot of time trying to unravel the facts.

CHAPTER II

A TOWER AND

A CONFUSION OF WORDS

One of the most familiar stories in the biblical tradition, that of the Tower of Babel (we really should say Babylon, though the outcome makes us want to have fun with "Babel"), now brings us almost to the end of these tales of the earliest world according to Israel's traditional culture. It is a story with a number of layers of significance.

11   ¹The whole Earth had one language and few words. ²And it happened, as they were wandering in the east,ᵃ and they found a valley in the land of Shin'ar, and they settled there. ³And they said to one another, "Come on, let's make bricks and burn them hard." And they had bricks for stone and pitch served them as mortar. ⁴And they said, "Come on, let's build ourselves a city and a tower with its top in Sky, and let's make a name for ourselves, lest we be scattered all over Earth." ⁵And Yahweh came down to see the city and the tower which the humans had built. ⁶And Yahweh said, "Look, it's one people and they all have one language, and this is only the beginning of what they will do. And now nothing they intend to do will be impossible for them. ⁷Come on, let's go down and 'confuse' their language there, so that no one

will be able to understand what another says." ⁸And Yahweh scattered them from there all across Earth, and they stopped building the city. ⁹Therefore its name is called Babel, because there Yahweh 'confused' the language of the whole Earth. And Yahweh scattered them from there all across Earth.

It seems almost as if somebody plopped this story down in the wrong place in the sequence. We have just looked at the lists of generations of descendants from Nōach's sons and how they were dispersed across that part of the world that Israelites knew anything about. But suddenly we are told that "the whole world" was wandering "in the east" and came into Shin'ar, southern Mesopotamia. Not only are they said to have had one language, but they are all together. The discrepancy from the dispersal in chapter 10 is immense, and it is not immediately comprehensible or even sensible. Should this story not precede the prior chapter? Well, perhaps it should, but it doesn't, and I'm not going to take it on myself to move things around like that. There may be a way to make sense of it, and I will wait until later to propose it.

Linguists and other scholars of the ancient world have puzzled over the question whether there was one Original Language, what the Germans call an *Ursprache*. Did they get the idea from this story? "The whole world had one language and few words." Of course, in terms of the sequence of stories here, the notion of a single original language from which the others all somehow split off comes easily out of the fact that, as they saw it, the whole world was populated after the Flood from three brothers, who must have spoken the same language. To be sure, there was that wife of Qayin, who might have spoken some other language, as we have no clue as to her parentage, and the wives of his descendants also presumably had some other language(s), unless the entire descendance was incestuous. That seems to be a speculation that did not occur to these storytellers. Having not troubled to scout out the origins of Qayin's wife, they left the matter to lie.

That later linguists divided the languages of the Near East into Semitic, Hamitic, and Japhethitic (to give them their Englished names) does not mean that the storytellers of these chapters had any such thing in mind. Linguists can do whatever they wish with their materials and let the ethnic historians grumble that this group among the Chamites spoke a Semitic or an Indo-European language, and therefore the biblical genealogical structure was wrong. Well, of course it was wrong. Just for starters, 'Asshūr is listed in chapter 10 as a descendant both of Cham and of Shem. There might be some ways to justify that by some speculations of facts we do not know, but as it stands, one of those designations of descendance must be wrong. It is lore—folklore, if you like—and folklore may very well more often be right than some of us may think, but it is seldom absolutely factually right. The argument over whether there was a single original language persists right up to now; during the week I was writing this I read a review of a linguistic book that mentioned some contemporary scholars who have opinions on both sides of the question. I don't mean to suggest that they accept the biblical view of the matter. If there was a single, original language (which I myself doubt), it would have begun splitting apart hundreds of thousands if not more than a million years before the implications of this. We're looking at stories composed quite recently in the long view of the human race. You will by now not be surprised, I expect, that I do not believe that the world was created in 4004 B.C.E.

But we can start from the point made above, that the narrative assumes that everybody was descended from three brothers, who must have spoken the same language. The story adds "and few words," which lends force to the thought that languages began very simply. Some would urge grunts at various pitches, which might convey "Food!" or "Lion!" or "Wow, look at that hunk" (or "chick, " whichever you prefer). Then such things turned somehow into words, but not many, and as time went on the human experience brought needs for more words and more complex combinations and more subtle ways of saying what needed to be said. And you end up with Aeschylus and Dante and Shakespeare and language-users of that stature. Well, maybe, though it is a well-observed fact of linguistic development that ancient languages were grammatically more complex than their modern descendants.

Think at least briefly of forms of the English verb and try to remember the last time you heard someone say "Thou didst" or "Ye are come," except in church quoting the King James Bible.

If languages tend, except under the influence of other languages, to become in some ways simpler, it is a reasonable thought that the earliest languages might have been more complex than they later became. That is a theoretical thought, because we do not know anything real about the language that the ancestors of the Israelites were speaking in, say, 2000 B.C.E., though we can know a fair amount about the languages of the Babylonians and the Egyptians, and a few other folks who left written documents. We can guess at what its linguistic family might have been, and how it was related to the languages in the Near East that were being written in 2000 B.C.E. But remember that 2000 is probably 3,000 years after Mesopotamia began to be inhabited by the folks who later were known as Sumerians, Akkadians, and others.

All right, let's get over to the folks in our story. They had a single language with few words, and they were wandering "in the east." East means east of Israel—never forget where this story was being told. I remarked above that this is a strange leap backwards, it seems. But if we are not to conclude that somebody simply put the tale down in the wrong place, there might be another explanation. Perhaps, like the two creation stories and the two Flood stories, we actually have two distinct accounts of the spread of humans across Earth after the Flood, and we shouldn't necessarily expect to find them at all similar.

Having one language, the people in our tale could speak with one another: "Come on, let's burn bricks." Good sense to use the material at hand, and in the Mesopotamian valley there was a lot of very good clay from which to make bricks. Mesopotamia, after all, means "land between rivers," and the rivers were the Tigris, more easterly, and the Euphrates. Rivers tend to deposit clay, especially if, as in Mesopotamia, they flood fairly frequently.

But the Israelite storytellers got in a bit of a dig at these brick-makers, and you can hear the Israelite audience tittering at the information. "They had bricks for stone, and pitch served them as mortar."

From the standpoint of the storytellers, bricks were a slovenly substitute for stone, which was the building material of choice in Palestine. No matter how hard you burned bricks, they were still a lesser building material than good Canaanite stone in Israelite opinion (and you also mustn't forget who is telling the story). The brick-makers had pitch, a naturally occurring bitumen, often almost liquid, for mortar. Israelites knew how to mix mortar for stone buildings that would hold together forever. Some of it is still holding in Palestine, maybe three thousand years later. It's not that Israelites did not use bricks. They did, but they knew better than to use them for really large buildings.

So these wanderers in Shin'ar want to cease being wanderers, and they set out not only to build a city with brick but an enormous tower "with its top in Sky." Their reason for doing this kind of thing is to give them a "name," fame and renown (recall the "renowned men," literally "men of name" in 6.4), and to prevent their being "scattered all over Earth." The fame is somewhat like Qayin's wife: who was there, besides "the whole Earth," to render renown to them? The worry about being scattered may be a clue that this story ought to precede chapter 10 rather than following it. But let us accept it as part of the worry in any case. Perhaps the Israelites thought that cities were an improvement on nomadism, that the power held by a concentrated population was safer than that of wandering families or clans. Or perhaps, as I will suggest later, this story was composed at a time when the safety of Israelites in their home territory was not very great—or even nonexistent. Clearly the wanderers in Shin'ar are interested in security. And that, in my opinion, is the best explanation for this tower.

But the question is, what might be a source of danger to "the whole Earth" (certainly meaning its population)? Some interpretations have seen the tower as an effort to invade the deity's space in heaven and have wanted to connect it with the Temple of Marduk, the tutelary god of Babylon. In that case, the threat might come from more powerful deities than Marduk—and Israelites could quite easily think of a candidate. But the word for "tower," *migdol*, has to do more with a defense tower, a fortress,[b] than with a temple or an invasive construction. Clearly the "name," the renown, if you like, is important, and a tower reaching up to Sky (remember not to think of Sky as heaven) will reinforce it by being impenetrable. They think that even a god (or gods) won't be able to trouble them there, and they will be safe from being scattered.

But Yahweh takes a little sight-seeing trip to Shin'ar—and why not? Deities like to get a close-up view now and then. Remember the evening stroll in the garden. But the intent is clear. The unity of these people—all relatives and speaking the same language—has its dangers. "This is only the beginning," and "nothing that they intend to do will be impossible for them." These people just might succeed in making themselves inaccessible in this tower to Yahweh's control or discipline, might become invulnerable and able to accomplish anything they wish within it. That almost suggests that Yahweh has at least a doubt about his omnipotence. Something else, it seems, is threatening to go wrong with the youthful world, and once again, forethought has failed to predict it. Perhaps we may expect to read of another flood, or perhaps an earthquake or a fire—at least some catastrophic damage that stops all this from happening. Well, not a flood; that has been promised.

But if forethought has failed him before, it does not again. Yahweh has seen the tower and the city, and ponders it. He concludes that there is a danger for the Earth in this project, and the question is whether he can forestall it. Yahweh turns out on this occasion to be more subtle than he has been before. He has in Flood 1 promised that he would not again destroy everything. Perhaps he wishes he had not made the promise, but he cannot now give it up. He does not relinquish his control of things, but he solves what he sees as the problem of human unity—which makes building the tower possible—in a somewhat humorously understated way. He "confuses" the single language, so that people cannot understand each other to give orders or carry them out. Even the "few words" that they are said to have had become unintelligible. And—are you surprised?—there is another pun here. "Let us 'confuse' [*balal*] their language." "Therefore its name is called Babel." The two words are not the same word, even though we have an English verb, "babble," which probably imitates babies' ways of "talking." Nor does "Babel" mean anything like "babble." It is Babylon, and it means something like "gate of El (god)." So not only is Yahweh's solution to the human unity of speech and ancestry humorous, but the telling of the story with its pun would surely have brought a chuckle if not a guffaw from the audience. And it comes out to exactly what the people intended to avoid by building the tower: their being scattered over Earth. We have already seen some considerable detail in chapter 10 about who they were and, by implication, where they had gone.

There is another linguistic point to be noticed about this confusion of languages. Yahweh states the intention by saying, "Come on, let us go down and confuse their language." There is that plural pronoun again, as it was in the first creation story and in the meeting at the end of chapter 3: "The man has become like one of us." That one might be less plausible than this one as an instance of the royal "we." But I doubt the royal "we" here too.

Notice, moreover, that this city with its intended monstrous tower was Babylon. I have referred to the idea that the tower meant the great temple of Marduk, who was Babylon's tutelary deity. I obviously think not. "Tower" (*migdol*) tends not to mean "temple" but, as I proposed, "defense," even "fortress." The issue is not a contest between two gods, but a contest of humans, indeed "the whole world," against Yahweh. If it had been a competition between gods, that competition and its participants would surely have been mentioned. But Yahweh had referred to the tower only as a place where humans as humans could do anything they wished.

There was, however, a real historical contest between Babylon and Israel, most obviously expressed in the fact that the Babylonians (properly Chaldeans, who were at that time the rulers in Babylon) invaded the Kingdom of Judah in the early sixth century B.C.E. (c. 586), destroyed the Jerusalem temple, seriously damaged the city, and exiled leading elements of the population of Judah to Babylonian territory, where they remained until Cyrus II of Persia permitted the Judean exiles to return home in the early 530s B.C.E. This permission is narrated in the Book of Ezra. Not all Jews did return to Palestine, and a Babylonian settlement of Jews continued for centuries, becoming a center of Jewish learning that resulted in the enormous rabbinic collection on practically everything of Jewish observance, the Babylonian Talmud.

One of the things we have in the story of the Tower of Babel is a nice bit of political humor as well. I already pointed out how the story ridicules the Babylonian building materials next to Israelite materials, brick against stone; and, of course, there was little if any stone in Mesopotamia. But Babel became for Jews the epitome of human grandiose exaggeration ("gate of god," indeed!) and with this tale also became the location of human linguistic variety, and the occasion for the breaking up of the post-Flood unity of ancestry as well. In fact, this story may almost function as a counterpart to the Flood in its less drastic explanation of the interruption of human efforts to maintain themselves as the arbiters of their own actions. Where the Flood started from the universality of what the story called "evil" and "spoiling" and solved it by destruction, the tower starts from the apparent unanimity of language and concentration on safety from dispersal and breaks it up by the disruption of linguistic unity, with the result of precisely the "scattering" that the tower was intended to prevent.[c] The story, then, is part of two different double stories. It is, as I proposed before, a double of the dispersal of nations from Nōach's sons in chapter 10, but also, as the story of an undertaking that had to be stopped, a double of the Flood story. Perhaps it is after all not in the wrong place.

An important critical position on the documents that went to make up the book of Genesis and the four following books holds that this story was part of what was almost surely the earliest of the documents—dated by Harold Bloom,[d] an important literary scholar, to the time of Solomon (died c. 925 B.C.E.). I very much incline, however, to date the tower story, at least in its final form, at or shortly after the time of the Exile, in the 580s to 530s B.C.E.—remember to count backwards— a time when Jews had seen Babylon at first hand and could vent some "told you so!" humor at the expense of a Babylon then itself conquered by the Persians. At the very least, a hypothetical earlier story involving the building of a large tower might have been modified in the sixth century to refer to Babylon. What an earlier story might have been, and what modifications were introduced, cannot now be disentangled. But I have my doubts about the whole construct of the so-called Documentary Hypothesis[e] of the composition of Genesis–Deuteronomy. Our European habit of thinking of everything as having existed in writing is in my judgment mistaken. I think that in these chapters we are looking at tales that circulated as oral tales, spoken, told, not read. To be sure, the tales came to be collected together and written down; otherwise we would not have them to read. I am actually grateful for that.

CHAPTER 12

A TRANSITIONAL GENEALOGY

Here comes the last genealogy in these chapters (do I hear sighs of relief?), which takes us to Abram, later renamed Abraham, who begins what passes as Israel's history. Like so many of the earlier stories, this one ends with material that looks forward. I am less convinced than some scholars that much of the Abraham story is historical rather than legendary, but for our present purposes that doesn't matter. We'll not go into that story, except the very beginning part of it that is still in chapter 11.

11   [10]These are the generations of Shem. Shem was 100 years old when he sired 'Arpakhshad two years after the flood. [11]Shem lived after he sired 'Arpakhshad 500 years and sired sons and daughters.[a]

[12]And 'Arpakhshad lived 35 years, and he sired Shelach. [13]And 'Arpakhshad lived after he sired Shelach 403 years and sired sons and daughters.

[14]And Shelach lived 30 years, and he sired 'Ēber. [15]And Shelach lived 403 years after he sired 'Ēber and sired sons and daughters.

[16]And 'Ēber lived 34 years, and he sired Peleg. [17]And 'Ēber lived after he sired Peleg 430 years and sired sons and daughters.

[18]And Peleg lived 30 years, and he sired Rᵉⁱū. [19]And Peleg lived after he sired Rᵉⁱū 209 years and sired sons and daughters.

[20]And Rᵉⁱū lived 32 years, and he sired Sᵉrūg. [21]And Rᵉⁱū lived after he sired Sᵉrūg 207 years and sired sons and daughters.

[22]And Sᵉrūg lived 30 years, and he sired Nachōr. [23]And Sᵉrūg lived after he sired Nachōr 200 years and sired sons and daughters.

[24]And Nachōr lived 29 years, and he sired Terach. [25]And Nachōr lived after he sired Terach 119 years and sired sons and daughters.

[26]And Terach lived 70 years, and he sired Abram, Nachōr, and Haran.

[27]These are the generations of Terach. Terach sired Abram, Nachōr, and Haran, and Haran sired Lōt. [28]And Haran died before Terach, his father, in the land of his birth, in Ūr of the Kasdîm.[b] [29]And Abram and Nachōr took wives. Abram's wife was named Sarai, and Nachōr's wife was named Milkah, the daughter of Haran, the father of Milkah and of Yiskah. [30]Now Sarai was barren; she had no. . . .[c] [31]And Terach took Abram his son and Lōt, Haran's son, his grandson, and Sarai, his daughter-in-law, the wife of Abram, his son, and they went with them[d] from Ūr of the Kasdîm, to go to the land of Kᵉnaʿan. And they came to Charan[e] and settled there. [32]And Terach's days were 205 years, and Terach died in Charan.

We need not pause long over this genealogy, as it leads up to the next phase of the story of Israel's beginnings, into which I will not go. It goes back to Shem, Nōach's son, whom we last saw some hundreds of years back and before the account of repopulating the Earth and the tower-building experiment that resulted in re-speeching the Earth. We have already seen several of the names earlier in the story, and it becomes interesting only with the birth of Terach. You probably noticed how much like the genealogy in chapter 5 (see Chapter Six) this one is in its style and its form, and perhaps you noticed also that, unlike chapter 5, it does not mention the deaths of the individuals or their ages at death.

We learn that Terach was in the city of Ur, a very famous and very ancient city, founded probably even earlier than the Sumerians, perhaps as early as 5000 B.C.E. It became one of the most influential cities of the Sumerian culture. Ur fell into less significant circumstances during the 1700s, and remained so until the Chaldeans came to power in Babylonia, at about 600 B.C.E.., when it was raised to more importance once again. That explains why the Judean storytellers referred to it as Ur of the Kasdîm—the name they called the Chaldeans. No love was lost between Judeans and Chaldeans because of the situation of invasion and exile, though we know of no underground or scurrilous meaning of *Kasdîm*. But it is especially interesting that the city Abram and his family left to go to Kᶜnaᶜan (Canaan) came to be associated in the tradition with the Chaldeans. One of the reasons for naming the city of Abram's origin as Chaldean suggests that if the major early ancestor of Israel was told to leave the Chaldeans to receive Kᶜnaᶜan from Yahweh, then the exiled Judeans in the sixth century B.C.E. might follow his example. Of course, when the Persians invaded and conquered the Chaldeans, Cyrus II's decree that the Jews could return from Babylonia succeeded in exactly that. The symbolic significance of Ur might very well have held, whether this genealogy came to be told during the Exile or after it.

Another element of the story that points forward is that Sarai, Abram's wife, was barren. That too was a factor overcome later, not without pain and sorrow. Of course, as every Israelite knew that Abraham and Sarah were the parents whose descendants were the Israelites themselves, this barrenness would be a serious obstacle to the very existence of Israel. And you will notice that in this first mention, neither Abram nor Sarai has the name by which he or she later became better known: Abraham and Sarah. For that, you'll have to read on beyond chapter 11.

So we have come from the "beginning" to the beginning of a new phase of the story, a phase that can begin to be called Israelite,[f] as opposed to the chapters we have looked at, which have rather to do with *'adam*, humans in general. The tale is quite mixed, much of it having to do with false starts and wrong decisions, with very good things that go bad, and with a point at which the continuance of the creation is in doubt, the subject of the divine regret. Not that everything gets that much better with the second start after the Flood. Curses on relatives continue to be pronounced and apparently approved by the deity, and the humans set out to seal themselves off from divine influence. The result is that the human condition has become permanent division, the problem of understanding, as it depends on language and speech, being, as it seems, insoluble. Perhaps Yahweh's solution to the problem of human unity and independence posed by the tower was understated, minimally destructive, and even somewhat humorous. But its outcome, as we see in our own day, remains sufficiently intractable to be nothing less than dangerous.

"And Elohîm saw all that he had made, and, there, it was very good." Was it? And were all of its subsequent problems and failures to be laid at human feet? That is one of the questions that must be considered in pondering this particular account of Earth's and humanity's origins.

CODA

(Italian, from Latin, *cauda*, tail)

So, at the end, not another tale but a tail. This one surely will not wag the dog, but it might brush aside a few flies.

You may wonder what I hoped would be the outcome for readers of this tour through Genesis 1–11. Much depends on where you were when you started. If you started from little or no prior experience of reading from the Bible, I hope that you found it engaging and interesting. No doubt some stories were more interesting than others, and I have no high hopes for the genealogies. But perhaps you have lost some fear or distaste at reading such things. At the very least, you now know that if you feel the need, you can skip parts. Perhaps, having survived a meeting with some Hebrew words and their meanings, you may be courageous enough to go further with this old Hebrew book.

If you started from familiarity with the stories because you were a regular reader of the Bible or a regular attender in a church or synagogue, then I begin by hoping you found some surprises. Some of them may have come from translations that were different from the ones you find familiar. More surprises might have come from the ways in which I proposed how the tales worked and what they implied. Because some of these proposals go in such very different directions from what you would ever have heard in sermons or in Sunday or synagogue school classes, they may have shocked you somewhat, perhaps especially the rather bold declaration that I think the Hebrew Bible is not a monotheistic book. I made those proposals, I assure you, not in order to shock you but because I think that what I have said about these stories is actually there.

I noted in the Introduction that I was amazed at how much I had seen in Genesis 1–11 that I had never seen before. Quite a number of instances are presented in some detail in the essays of reading. The result is that the more I think about these tales, the more impressed I am by their antiquity and by their home in the Hebrew language before the start of the Common Era. I said that I think there is no Final Truth about these stories—no Truth we can find that will bring all conversation about them to a stop. That would require that someone discover everything to be discovered in them, which in my opinion is simply not in the nature of stories, modern or ancient, English, Arabic, Chinese, or Hebrew.

Sometimes stories, in effect, wear out, having told us all that we can take in. I wonder how close at least some of these are to that stage. I suspect that the time will come when they reach it. Perhaps we hasten that time by the eagerness with which the established religions, Christianity foremost, insist on believing them. What they mean by believing varies from one religious group to another, and ranges from a level of literal and provable truth, like the science that is so central to our culture, all the way to the level that finds them giving us insight into some interesting human problems. Frankly, I hope you may be closer now to not believing them in the ways of the first, literalistic sort. If we are not somehow required to believe, then perhaps we can more readily search out what the tales say and how they say it (those two matters are equally important), and what that means for us.

Some of what they say is surely worth thinking about: believing too implicitly in what a snake tells you, for instance—the way Adam but not Chavah did—had some outcomes that might better have been avoided. But don't look too closely for moral lessons here. Even the deities in these stories may not be the best guides to behavior. And in any case, stories—any stories—may seldom be there in order to teach lessons of that sort.

One of the things that strikes me now about these tales—and I have been reading and hearing them since I was a little boy, more years ago than I wish to admit—is that they are not really ours in the ways, for instance, that Coyote stories belong to American Indians, or the "Thousand and One Nights" belong to Arabic-speaking people. These tales from the Bible have been supposed to be ours mostly because the principal religions in our culture certify them as guides to behavior and truths to be believed. I worry a bit that the status of these tales has kept some others from becoming the stories that we might find explain us. I don't mean that awful moralistic one whose punch line is "I cannot tell a lie." I quite envy cultures that actually have and know their own stories. I'm not going to suggest any candidates for our list, but I hope you would have gotten a yen for stories with bite and taste to them, and that you might think of some we could take up or some we already have that would qualify. I'd be glad to hear about them.

I enjoyed the process of thinking and writing this book, and I enjoyed the tales too as I encountered them in quite new ways. Thank you for coming along.

Notes

a. The traditional phrase, "In the beginning," runs afoul of the way the first word, *bᵉrēshît*, arranges its vowels. To translate "in the beginning," the word ought to be *barēshît*. As it stands, the word is closer to "in beginning of," which needs an object. That object should be "Elohîm's creating," which necessitates modifying the finite verb form *bara'*, "created," in a past tense, into an infinitive, *bᵉrō'*. These very minor changes are only to the vowel signs, introduced into the biblical text in the Middle Ages. I have no scruples against changing them, unlike the problem of changing the consonants.

b. The phrase "shapeless and empty," *tōhū wabōhū*, is a fixed phrase, doubtless because of its rhyming, assonantal quality. It seems to refer to something like a blob.

c. The tendency of Christian versions to translate "wind," *rūach*, as "spirit" is an intrusion of Trinitarian theology into a non-Trinitarian book. The word usually, as here, means "wind" or "breath."

d. "Day one" is a somewhat odd expression, but to say "first day" would have required a different expression. The other days all have the ordinal form of the number. And notice that the day began with evening, as the Jewish understanding of the day still does. I wonder whether that manner of reckoning arose from this depiction of creation in which darkness was present before light. Perhaps it came from the Israelite use of a lunar calendar, where calculations would begin from sunset.

e. The word "bowlshape" continues a pattern that extends throughout this story: an abstract term that is then named as a familiar phenomenon. In the abstract, "bowlshape" seems to signify a hemispherical shape, here placed upside down. It is solid, separating one body of water from another.

f. The term "creep" is not really applicable to sea-dwelling creatures, but the Israelites were not a seagoing people. The same word turns up among the land-dwelling beings in vv. 24–25, doubtless meaning small beasts like rats, and perhaps snakes. What the neighboring Phoenicians, who were great sailors, would have called this sea-dwelling group of animals is not known, but Israelites could doubtless have asked them.

g. "There now" is usually translated "Behold," but I fail to see a necessary connection in the word to sight. It is rather an exclamation that simply calls attention to something, and I get weary enough of repeated "beholds" to want something different. See also 3.22. We might think of it as an almost shouted exclamation, "Hey!!"

h. The word "history" is more literally "generations," but it is so often used to designate a series of events, and since in this chapter there are no births or successive generations of people, I have used the more applicable English term. The word recurs in 11.10, and there, because what follows is genealogical, I have translated it as "generations."

CHAPTER 2

a. The fact that *shoham* stone is listed along with gold and bdellium, a precious gem, suggests that it was a now unidentifiable precious stone.

b. We know that river as Euphrates, a Greek version of the name.

c. The expression "facing him" literally means something like "as one in front of him," in effect, corresponding to him.

d. For the first time, our male human is referred to without a definite article, and we can call him Adam. Perhaps I can spoil the relief of a name that looks familiar by saying that it should be pronounced "Ah-dahm" (accent on the second syllable).

e. I say that *Yahweh* "may have been pronounced" because we never see the Hebrew consonants of that name with the vowels that originally belonged to it. Therefore, we do not really know how the ancients pronounced it. Martin Buber, the famous Jewish thinker, thought that it should be Yahū, and he explained a meaning for the name in that form. He has not had many followers, though *yahu* occurs as a combination form in names such as Elijah (Hebrew, eliyahū). The evidence for pronouncing the name as Yahweh is entirely from some Greek sources that spelled it approximately *iaoue*, which comes very close to the Hebrew. The first *h* should be lightly pronounced. If the name was pronounced "Yahweh," it was probably a verbal form meaning something like "he causes to be," which may have tones of "he acts." Not many deities among the world's religions have been named as verbs.

f. The verb "forming" is often used for shaping pottery.

g. The standard edition of the Hebrew Bible sets this in poetic form, but most manuscripts do not. The poetic form is derived from analysis, and there might be more than one possible form of it.

h. But in the Flood story, chapters 6.19–20 and 7.2–3, these words are used for the pairs of animals going into Nōach's ship.

CHAPTER 3

a. The word "permanently" is often translated as "forever," which has a very specific and familiar meaning in our culture, but which may not have been a concept the ancient Israelites had. That it means what we mean by "forever" is not at all likely. Mostly the word means something close to "a long time"; it can be either past or future, and its extent is usually not stated. I've translated it as "permanently" here with some trepidation.

CHAPTER 4

a. The text is somewhat damaged here. At some point in the copying, a scribe omitted writing down what Qayin said, and nobody noticed. Later copyists had to write exactly what was in front of them, so the omission is still there. It was probably some sort of suggestion that they go out to the country.

b. Qayin's name is probably related to a verb of somewhat alarming meaning—*qyn*, "to sing a dirge." Perhaps the pun with *qanah*, "gotten," was part of a tendency to give a positive spin to a birth, but it might also have been intended to take the reader's mind away from the proper etymology. Ancient readers of Hebrew knew their language better than we do, and it seems likely that they would have seen the connection.

c. In Steinbeck's novel the main character, whose name is Adam, is dying at the end of the book, and his last word is a version of the Hebrew word here, *timšel* (the biblical text reads *timšol*, but I do not criticize Steinbeck on that account).

d. I have not commented on Hebel's name, and it is perhaps slightly surprising that the storytellers did not introduce a pun. The word is the same as the term used somewhat as a key word in the book of Ecclesiastes (Hebrew name, Qoheleth). There *hebel habalîm* is usually translated "Vanity of vanities," meaning something empty of significance, not something that people falsely parade to raise others' opinions of them. One of the connotations of the word is something like a puff of wind, which is gone almost before it is sensed. That is nearly what happens to Hebel.

CHAPTER 5

a. Isn't it interesting that faced with a statement like this, which doesn't make any sense—how does a man find a wife when there are no unrelated female people anywhere around?—we instantly want to think of a hypothetical scientific or historical answer to it? If Qayin was one of only three human beings on Earth, the other two being his parents, then the wife might have come from somewhere other than Earth. Talk about myth!

b. It is conceivable that the use of Elohîm here comes from the increasing sense among Jews of the holiness of the name Yahweh and their reluctance to pronounce it.

CHAPTER 6

a. Recall that the word 'adam means both a human being and, more generally, the human species, the race, if you like. Hence it can sometimes be given a plural reference, as in the pronouns here. To be sure, in ch. 1 Elohîm did not call Adam by that name, as there the word was a species designation.

CHAPTER 7

a. The Hebrew here says ha'dam, "the Adam," or as I have said it, "the humans," even though the noun is singular.

b. The verb behind the ellipsis occurs only here in the Hebrew Bible, and its meaning is simply not known.

c. I don't like "when" as a translation of the particle, which ordinarily means something more like "whom." In that case it might seem to be out of place in the sentence, because it would refer clear down to "them" at the very end of the sentence. I'm not sure how to rewrite my sentence to show that.

d. See my book *In Turns of Tempest: A Reading of Job with a Translation* (Stanford, 1990).

CHAPTER 8

a. Once more, though I have translated ha'adam in the plural, it is singular, and in the second part of the sentence I have left the singular "his" with "heart." The same is true of "the humans" in v. 7. Maybe I should be translating the word "the Adam." The reference seems to be to the whole race.

b. According to a standard dictionary of the Bible, a cubit in the period of the Hebrew Bible was the length of the arm from the elbow to the tip of the middle finger. As that length would vary from person to person, the size of a cubit might have been from about 17.5 to about 20 inches. So a 300-cubit ship would be in the range of 437.5 to 500 feet long. For the other dimensions, 50 cubits wide would be between 73 and 83 feet, and 30 cubits high would be 43.75 to 50 feet. People who know about good dimensions for ships would know approximately what this one's seaworthiness would likely be. The ship in the Gilgamesh Epic is 120 Mesopotamian cubits high and 120 cubits on each side of a square deck. That sounds to me like a very unhandy vessel. I have not discovered the length of the Babylonian cubit.

c. I have puzzled over the fact that the European and North American tradition of the New Year is January 1, in the middle of winter. More naturally, for us, the year would begin in the spring, perhaps the end of February or early March. And what do you know, there is evidence that it once did. Think of the names of the last months of the year in English—September, October, November, and December—all derived from Latin numerals, seventh, eighth, ninth, and tenth. That suggests that our current first and second months were once the eleventh and twelfth, which might bring our earlier New Year around to approximately when the Near Eastern year began, at least in the counting of its months.

d. Something else is required for truly "kosher" meat nowadays, namely, a properly certified person doing the slaughtering.

CHAPTER 10

a. The phrase reads "islands of the peoples," a strange way of referring to peoples who lived (mostly) on islands. But it does not make a whole lot of sense to say that the islands separated themselves. Perhaps in this case "separated" means something like "distinguished."

b. There seems something missing from this sentence, which is in an odd order and lacks any object of the passive verb "was born."

c. The problem here is a singular verb, "was born," with a plural subject; another of those errors caught too late to be corrected in the copying.

d. Another pun. The verb for "divided" is a form of *palag*.

e. The name Mēsha may be Moabite, in the country east of the Jordan River (a famous inscription from a Moabite king by that name is an important historical document), but Saphar is not to be found. So most of the sons of Yoqtan of whom we know so little are not possible to locate with any assurance.

f. Many of these names are conjectural, made by scholars, and I will not attempt to specify the probability that the guess is correct.

g. Ezekiel 38–39 describes a powerful king, Gōg of Magōg, who was bringing destruction to Israel from the north, which often meant from Asia Minor (modern Turkey). In Revelation 20.8 we find two monstrous enemies named Gog and Magog, which may simply be a misunderstanding of Ezekiel—not the first misunderstanding of that difficult book.

h. The Ionians were a Greek-speaking people.

i. Some scholars identify Tiras with the Etruscans, who lived in Italy before the Romans. That seems doubtful, though the consonants of the name provide a reason some find plausible.

j. Tarshîsh was a mysterious place, located far to Israel's west. Some even locate it in Spain, because a later Roman city there was named Tartessus. "Ships of Tarshîsh" in the Bible were apparently oceangoing ships, but where they went if they went to Tarshîsh is simply unknown. The prophet Jonah, told to go east to Nineveh, got on a ship to go to Tarshîsh, perhaps as far west as one could go. He never got there, having been interrupted by that large fish (not, by the way, a whale).

k. The name Dōdanîm is unknown, but some scholars want to change the first *D* to an *R*. The two letters in Hebrew look quite similar and were fairly often confused in copying. Rōdanîm would connect these people to the island of Rhodes. I am not willing to change consonants, even if the idea in this case is plausible.

l. Kūsh is a difficult one. The name is given anciently to Ethiopia, some distance down the east coast of Africa. That would make some sense of its connection to Cham, as the other names of his descendants seem mostly to be somewhere in Africa. But there was also an area known as Kūsh that doesn't seem to be in that area, such as its occurrence in Genesis 2, the location of one of the rivers. A people living southeast of Mesopotamia, known as the Kassites, conquered the Babylonian area for a time in the second millennium B.C.E., and that is another possible identity for Kūsh.

m. Mitsrayim is Egypt. Interestingly, the name of Mitsrayim is a dual form of the noun, meaning "two." Egypt was formed fairly early in its history by a union of what were named Upper Egypt and Lower Egypt, giving rise to the dual form of the name.

n. It is noticeable that no descendants of Pūt were listed.

o. Sh^eba' is hard to disentangle from S^eba'. It is best known from Solomon's acquaintance with a queen of the group.

p. Nimrōd is described somewhat obscurely as a "mighty hunter before Yahweh," and the subject of an apparently proverbial comparison. More than that we do not know. But Nimrōd is credited with being the founder of the major empires of southern Mesopotamia in the second millennium B.C.E. (that is, 2000–1000 B.C.E.).

q. 'Erekh is the Hebrew form of a city anciently known as Uruk, a very important early city, where Gilgamesh, the hero of the Epic of Gilgamesh, one of the great literary works of the ancient world, was king, if he was historical, in the third millennium B.C.E. (3000–2000).

r. Shin'ar is the name not of a group of people but of a territory, pretty much the southern Mesopotamian territory ruled by the Akkadians and the Babylonians.

s. Asshūr was Assyria, the empire in northern Mesopotamia that invaded the northern Israelite kingdom in the eighth century B.C.E. and led to the "lost tribes of Israel" being dispersed as captives in Assyria. Oddly, 'Asshūr appears also as a descendant of Shem. That may reflect something mixed about 'Asshūr, but the list-makers seldom doubled anybody.

t. The Israelite ethnographers seem to have assumed that R^echōbōt-'îr was a separate city, but as the word *r^echōbōt* may mean something like "squares," the term might refer to a district of Nîn^evēh, perhaps called "City squares."

u. There seem to be two groups named Lūd or Lūdîm (plural form), one a descendant of Mitsrayim (Egypt), the other a descendant of Shem. If they were two different groups, this one may have been in north Africa, west of Egypt.

v. Pᵉlishtîm signifies the Philistines. A wrong word placement leads to an erroneous statement: the Kaphtōrîm signifies the inhabitants of the island of Crete, and it was traditionally from Crete that the Pᵉlishtîm came to Palestine. The Philistines, long-term enemies of the Israelites, apparently came somewhat late to Palestine. The Romans used the Philistine name for the whole province. Since the text says that they came from the territory of the Kasluchîm, an unknown group, it seems that at some point some copyist reversed that group with the Kaphtōrîm.

w. The inhabitants of the island of Crete are called in this list both the Kaphtōrîm and the Kittîm.

x. Chēt is the same as Hittites, the famous culture and kingdom in central Asia Minor in the latter part of the second millennium B.C.E. But these folks seemingly were not related to those Hittites. Otherwise they are unknown.

y. ʾᴱmorî or Amorites were a considerable group of people who went all over Mesopotamia and Syria in the second millennium B.C.E. They apparently kept some ethnic identity but had no specific territory.

z. On ʾAsshūr see note s. ʾAsshūr is listed also as a descendant of Nimrōd, the "mighty hunter" among Cham's descendants.

aa. Lūd is another duplication. One of Egypt's (Mitsrayim's) descendants is Lūdim (see note u) and was probably a north African group. This Lūd is sometimes thought to be the Lydians, a Greek-speaking group in western Asia Minor, an identity doubted by many.

bb. ʾᴬram or Aramaeans was the Syrians, centered on Damascus. The indigenous name of the country we now call Syria is Aram. The Aramaeans were certainly some of Israel's ancestors. Deuteronomy 26.5 quotes a ritual pronouncement to be made on entry into the promised land, which starts, "My father was a wandering Aramaean."

cc. The usual English spelling of ʿŪts is Uz, and this is the homeland of Job. Exactly where in the Arabian area it was is not known.

dd. ʿĒber is the origin of the term Hebrew. It is a name that appears a number of times in the Hebrew Bible.

ee. On Peleg see also note d in this chapter. It is suggested that Peleg was in Mesopotamia, and because his name is related to the word for "canal," he is associated with Mesopotamian irrigation. Perhaps the "world's being divided" in his time ("divided" is a pun on his name) points to the Tower of Babel story.

ff. Ōphîr was famous for its gold (Job 22.24, etc.), but no one knows certainly where it was. I Kings 9.28 says it is reached by ship, and various areas from India to the Arabian coast and north Africa have been proposed.

gg. In 2.11–12 Chᵃvîlah is described as surrounded by one of the rivers coming out of Eden, and as having gold of good quality. It seems that Yoqtan was connected to rich gold areas.

CHAPTER 11

a. "In the east" is not a literal translation. It actually says something closer to "from the east," but there are other places where the locative preposition does not seem to mean literally "from" one place to another, but has to do with being in an area.

b. I argued this interpretation of the tower as early as my book *Irony in the Old Testament* (Westminster Press, 1965; 2nd ed., Almond Press, 1981), p. 88. The interpretation came from a 1963 lecture at Stanford by the late Professor Abraham Joshua Heschel, to whom I have been indebted for much more than this.

c. Readers familiar with the Uncle Remus stories will notice that this tale is the reverse of "Bre'r Rabbit." Threatened with being thrown into the briar patch, Bre'r Rabbit protests loudly against it, though that is exactly what he wants to happen. The tower builders hope to avoid being scattered and fail.

d. Bloom's theory, which I find fascinating, but not finally believable, is in his book with David Rosenberg, *The Book of J* (Grove Weidenfeld, 1990), translated from the Hebrew by Rosenberg and interpreted by Bloom.

e. Scholars beginning in the eighteenth century noticed some of the differences I have pointed out both in detail and in style among various parts of the first five books of the Hebrew Bible, traditionally called the "Five Books of Moses" on the assumption that Moses wrote them. The observations of various differences coalesced into a supposition of four basic documents from which the five books were compiled: the one assumed to be the earliest designated "J" because it characteristically named the deity Yahweh (in German spelled *Jahweh*); a second one, perhaps compiled a century later, called "E," which used Elohîm for the deity; one called "D," consisting mostly of the book of Deuteronomy but also some editing in earlier parts that use what seems to be Deuteronomy's characteristic style, probably dated shortly before the Babylonian Exile; and the latest, called "P" from a bias toward priestly matters, dated usually after the Exile and including all of the detailed ritual laws, especially of Leviticus. In our eleven chapters, the second creation story, the garden of Eden, Qayin and Hebel, Flood 1, and the Tower of Babel are supposed to be "J," because they use Yahweh. There is no clear "E" or "D" material in these chapters, though an occasional odd fragment (possibly the story of the "sons of the Elohîm") might be identified by one or another scholar as "E." The first creation story, Flood 2, and the genealogies are usually identified as "P" material. Obviously, some of the differences that have given rise to the hypothesis are just what I have seen. It's simply that I doubt the idea of thoroughgoing written "documents" with specific dates ascribed to them. If I am right about the situation behind the

Tower of Babel story, then I can't date it in "J" in the tenth or ninth century B.C.E. The whole matter is complicated, and I have observed a weakening of this "Documentary Hypothesis" among scholars in recent years. More study on orally transmitted traditions in many cultures has modified an earlier supposition about the centrality of the written and edited word, and I have participated in that interest.

CHAPTER 12

a. It has been some time since we have seen clear reference to women. The reader can see that this genealogy is in the same basic format as the long one in Genesis 5. We can assume that its compilers and transmitters were in the same tradition as those responsible for ch. 5, though we do not really know what that tradition was. I incline to think that there were generations of "lore-masters" responsible for aspects of the traditional oral culture of Israel, perhaps even some who specialized in family and descendancy lore.

b. Kasdîm refers to the people we usually hear of as the Chaldeans, who ruled Babylonia in its last period of power, including the time of the Judean Exile there in the sixth century B.C.E. That event represented a turning point in the history of Israel, perhaps comparable to the Civil War in American history. It is interesting how we keep coming back to Babylon, having just been there in the Tower of Babel story. But in terms of the assumed but necessarily hypothetical date of Abraham's life (perhaps around 1800–1500 B.C.E.?), to call the city Ur of the Kasdîm is a quite massive anachronism. The Chaldeans were nowhere in sight at that early time.

c. Another textual problem. The word in the *ellipsis ought* to be *yeled*, "child," but it is *walad*, which unless it is a variant spelling of *yeled*, means nothing. I'm going to be true to my principles, and not change that first consonant, even though the Samaritan Pentateuch, an old and usually quite reliable text, gives evidence in favor of the change. So I'm stuffy and principled. Sorry. You can write in "child" if you wish.

d. The sentence is odd in its numbers. It says, "They went with them," and we can be sure that "they" were all those named before. Perhaps "with them" was a later error for "with him."

e. Charan was in northern Mesopotamia, on the best route to the Mediterranean coast and Palestine. The city's name is not at all like that of the then-dead Haran.

f. Actually, only when we get to Jacob later in Genesis can we talk about Israel, as that name was bestowed on Jacob in Gen. 35.10, and Jacob's sons gave their names to the twelve tribes of the later nation of Israel.